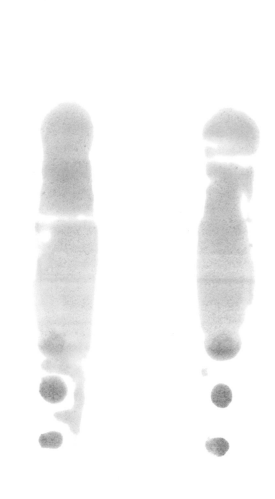

AIRCOM
Canada's Air Force

Enticingly beautiful British Columbia glacial terrain. Skimming the peaks and
ridges is a 442 Squadron SAR helicopter. In such country many a hapless flier
or hiker has become the focus of the 442 SAR experts.

Title page
The Lockheed T-33 has been on RCAF/CF strength since 1951. Here No. 174
flies on a training mission near CFB North Bay on June 26, 1991. It's in 414
(EW) Squadron's special 50th anniversary colour scheme that features its Black
Knight ("Sir Cedric") on the nose. Design was worked out among squadron
members and perfected by the base refinishers, headed by MCpl John Fraser.
Crewing 174 are Capts Richard Pulman, pilot, and Brad Mason, EWO. Capt
Lou Glussich was flying the photo T-bird:

AIRCOM
Canada's Air Force

By Larry Milberry

CANAV Books

Front endpaper

One of eight Sikorsky CH-124 Sea Kings modified for service in the Persian Gulf, 1990–91. Note the FLIR installation on the nose. The orange disc is the crash position indicator, a Canadian invention. Ahead of it is a radar warning receiver. Shot at Hamilton International Air Show, June 14, 1991

Back endpaper

The Snowbirds at the *Festival Aérien de Québec*, August 17–18, 1991: **1** The team, led by Maj Bob Stephan, is ready to taxi for a show. **2** Capts Bill Watts, Brooke Lawrence and Vince Jandrisch chatting it up just before strapping in. **3** Capts Jandrisch, Jeff Hill and Réal Turgeon sign autographs for eager fans. **4** The line abreast loop over Quebec City airport. **5** Capts Bill Watts (nearest, No. 6) and Glenn Oerzen (No. 8) dive through a loop over the mouth of the St. Charles River in downtown Quebec. **6** Line abreast, 5 Snowbirds fly down the St. Lawrence as a freighter steams upbound. **7** Capt Nick Cassidy holds his Tutor in tight formation over the St. Lawrence.

DESIGN
Robin Brass Studio, Toronto

KEYBOARDING
Jo-Ann Gordon/Pas de Deux, Toronto

PROOFREADING
Ralph Clint

PHOTO RETOUCHING
Stephen Ng/BNC Inc., Don Mills, Ont.

COLOUR SEPARATIONS AND FILM WORK
Advance Laser Graphic Arts (International) Ltd., Hong Kong

Printed and bound in Canada by the Bryant Press Ltd., Toronto

Published by
CANAV Books
Larry Milberry, Publisher
51 Balsam Avenue
Toronto M4E 3B6
Canada

Canadian Cataloguing in Publication Data

Milberry, Larry, 1943–
    AIRCOM: Canada's Air Force

Includes index
ISBN 0-921922-05-0

1. Canada. Canadian Armed Forces. Air Command.
2. Aeronautics, Military – Canada. I. Title

UG635.C2M55 1991   358.4'00971   C91-094788-0

A 444 "Cobra" Squadron Kiowa patrols along the Rhine at a border crossing between France and Germany, July 23, 1988.

CONTENTS

A Musketeer trainer of No.3 CFFTS banks over Manitoba farm country.

PREFACE

AIRCOM: Canada's Air Force is a special tenth-anniversary CANAV Books publication. It's the latest of the books covering military aviation in Canada. The flagship of the list is *Sixty Years: The RCAF and CF Air Command 1924–1984* from CANAV, which has also published *The RCAF at War 1939-1945* and *Canada's Air Force Today*. Another valuable title is John McQuarrie's *Canadian Wings* from McGraw-Hill Ryerson. No doubt the list will keep on growing.

AIRCOM brings the reader up-to-date with developments in the air force but also hearkens back to "the good old days" of the RCAF in its postwar heyday. It has much to offer readers young and old with an interest in military aviation.

Air Command Today

Air Command has recorded a great deal of history recently. By far the most important event was the war in the Persian Gulf. It began August 2, 1990 when Iraq invaded Kuwait. A few days later Canada agreed to send a flotilla to help enforce a United Nations trade embargo against Iraq. This involved HMCSs *Athabaskan, Terra Nova* and *Protecteur*—Task Group 302.3. The ships carried five specially modified Sea Kings that would prove valuable in locating and inspecting shipping in the Gulf. They made their first intercept on October 2 and by war's end on February 28 had logged nearly 30% of all shipping inspections conducted by the UN coalition. As well, *Protecteur* reprovisioned and refuelled her sister ships, maintained the Sea Kings, and refuelled many ships of various coalition navies. Task Group 302.3 arrived home in Halifax on April 7. Unfortunately, AIRCOM does not have coverage of the Sea Kings at war—during my visit to the Gulf, a trip out to the Canadian ships could not be arranged.

Canada's CF-18s also gave great service in the Gulf War. In the end, 26 were stationed at Doha in Qatar, beginning October 6. Crews from several Hornet squadrons pitched in and more than 5700 hours were safely flown. The CF-18s were part of CATGME—Canadian Air Task Group Middle East. Details of CATGME appear in *Canada's Air Force Today – 1991 Update* published by CANAV. The Gulf

Hornets were officially welcomed home with a big ceremony at CFB Ottawa on March 19.

Supporting the entire Canadian contingent in the Gulf was Air Transport Group. Its CC-130s and CC-137s maintained an aerial pipeline flying personnel, equipment and supplies from Canadian bases through to Lahr and Cyprus, then on to Bahrain and Qatar. This huge tasking came under Operation Scimitar (build-up stage), Operation Friction (sustainment stage) and other operations.

The Gulf conflict was the first time Canada had gone to war since Korea in 1950–53. Happily, the approximately 3600 Canadians who served in the Gulf all came home safely. They did an outstanding job, demonstrating the high degree of training, readiness and spirit always typical of Canada's soldiers, sailors and aviators.

While the Gulf War was a highlight, many other noteworthy factors have affected AIRCOM. The reality of budget cuts has been most prominent. There is a global trend towards reducing defence budgets. This is the direct result of the end of the Cold War, but also of huge national deficits. The symbolic dismantling of the Berlin Wall, the death of the Warsaw Pact, the rise of democracy in the USSR and its former client states, and a European renaissance have all led to an easing of international tensions. Meanwhile, decades of disarmament talks between the US and USSR are slowly bearing fruit in agreements to reduce nuclear and conventional forces. In May 1991 the US announced its unilateral ban on all chemical weapons.

For Canada, the new face of Europe certainly means a reduced NATO commitment. This was hinted at in Ottawa's February 1991 announcement that it was to disband 409 Squadron, one of Canada's CF-18 units in Germany. In June 1991 it was absorbed into the remaining two squadrons, 421 and 439. Another subtle clue came in January 1991 when No.1 Canadian Air Division ceased being part of Canadian Forces Europe and was placed under AIRCOM. A gradual reduction of Canada's 7,700-strong land and air NATO contingent in Germany is surely on the way.

Cutbacks are also coming at home, but these are more closely linked to the sorry state of the nation's economy. When times are tough, Ottawa looks first to the Department of National Defence to cut costs. This is an old story. In 1959 when it felt it could no longer justify spending on the RCAF's new Avro Arrow interceptor, the government axed the entire program. Thus, development and production spending worth probably $1 billion in 1959 dollars was curtailed. In 1971, the DND suffered a $1.8 billion budget reduction, in 1989 $2.8 billion and in May 1991 $900,000, just to mention some of the cuts.

Meanwhile Air Command has streamlined its operations by eliminating several fleets. These were costly to support, and it was a case of either scrapping them or spending millions to refurbish them. Thus, thought was given to revamping the Dakota fleet with a standardized cockpit and maybe even turboprop engines. A Tracker was tried with PT6s. The debate went on for years as to whether or not AIRCOM should modernize its Chinook fleet. After much study of all the pros and cons, the three fleets were retired in 1989, 1990 and 1991 respectively. Meanwhile, the 30-year-old Cosmopolitan fleet has been put through a modernization program and

aging fleets such as the CF-5s are steadily resuscitated through DLIR programs (depot level inspection and repair). Others, such as the Buffalo, Kiowa and T-33, will have to be retired as the costs of keeping them going become prohibitive.

Not all is gloom and doom, however. Although defence dollars are tighter than ever, AIRCOM has added a few aircraft and others are on the way. Five new CC-130 Hercules were delivered during the Gulf War. Four new Dash 8 navigation trainers have joined AIRCOM. These relieved four C-130s and let Air Transport Group make more productive use of the "Hercs". Plans call for the new C-130s to be converted for aerial refuelling of Fighter Group's CF-5s and CF-18s. There are tentative plans for 418 Air Reserve Squadron in Edmonton to play a part in this operation. Meanwhile, the Dash 8 fleet is being operated mainly by 402 Air Reserve Squadron in Winnipeg. With the announced re-formation of 434 Squadron on the east coast with T-33s and Challengers, 420 Air Reserve Squadron is expected to be reactivated to share in running the operation. This reflects implementation of the DND's "Total Force" philosophy whereby the regular force and the reserves work together more closely.

CF-5 No. 717 (call sign Rut Zulu) banks away from a 437 Squadron tanker after refuelling near Cold Lake, April 4, 1989.

Theoretically this will save taxpayers' dollars.

Three CP-140A Arcturus are being delivered to supplement Maritime Air Group's 18 ASW Auroras. Though not ASW capable, the Arcturus will carry out training, fisheries patrols, sovereignty patrols and SAR duties, relieving the Aurora fleet and allowing MAG to stretch airframe lives and spread out maintenance costs.

A huge upcoming fleet replacement for MAG involves the Sea King. Now that Maritime Command is taking delivery of its new CPFs (Canadian Patrol Frigates), the antiquated Sea Kings will have to go. The EH-101 helicopter, developed by a European consortium, has been touted in this multi-billion dollar program. However, it is expected that when the CPF goes on its initial patrol, it will still be carrying Sea Kings—new aircraft acquisitions seem to take forever. It was about nine years from establishment of the Long Range Patrol Aircraft (Argus replacement) management group to delivery of the first Aurora. It will be the late 1990s before MAG starts operating a new ASW helicopter.

Besides the paring of aircraft fleets, AIRCOM has been hit by the closing of CFB Summerside. This coincided with the demise of the Tracker fleet and reduction to paper squadron status of 880 and 420 Squadrons. Summerside's other unit, 413 SAR Squadron, moved to Greenwood in the summer of 1991. The downsizing and closure of other bases is sure to come as the 1990s progress. (CFBs Chatham and Toronto have already been removed from AIRCOM control and turned over to the army.)

AIRCOM is using two other approaches to save money and fleet wear and tear—contracting services and leasing airplanes. For some years ATG has been contracting air freight and passenger-carrying work. This began in the 1980s with Worldways DC-8s being hired. More recently, Nationair and Air Canada have been doing a lot of the flying previously done by ATG. In May 1991 Air Canada won a long-term contract to provide service on what for years was 437 Squadron's famous domestic schedule run: Shearwater–Trenton–Ottawa–Winnipeg–Edmonton (Namao)–Vancouver-Comox. The new Air Canada route will fly Halifax–Ottawa–Toronto–Winnipeg–Edmonton (International)–Vancouver. As civil air terminals will be used, this will greatly reduce the services provided by ATG's air movements units (AMUs) at Shearwater, Trenton, Ottawa, Winnipeg and Edmonton.

Using commercial carriers to serve the military is not unique to Canada. The USAF has a large civil standby fleet ready for emergencies. It was heavily used during the Gulf War. Britain's Ministry of Defence has also made wide use of the airlines.

In 1990 civil contractors took over Department of Fisheries and Oceans tasks on the east and west coasts using King Airs equipped with advanced radar and electronics. These replaced the Trackers on fisheries work. The same year AIRCOM leased its first aircraft, a pair of King Air 200s from Awood Air of Thunder Bay. The King Airs were needed by the Central Flying School in Winnipeg for multi-engine training previously done with the Dakota. AIRCOM has plans to turn over primary and multi-engine fixed-wing and rotary-wing training to a civil operator, so this trend of contracting and leasing appears to be here to stay.

Background to the Photos

AIRCOM is CANAV's 16th title since it published *The Avro CF-100* in 1981. Despite the small size of the Canadian book market and its ever-unpredictable response to any new book, a number of CANAV's titles have become bestsellers. *Sixty Years* reached its fifth printing, a landmark rarely achieved by a Canadian hardcover.

AIRCOM is something new from CANAV—its first purely photographic venture. It could be called an album and, as such, it is one of the grandest to focus on any modern air force. Besides more than 300 photos, the book offers much new data and AIRCOM "info" in its extensive captions. All the photos have been taken by me since 1959.

As people often ask how I got into aviation photography, this is a good place for a brief bio. My first camera was a plastic Tower 127 purchased about 1950 for $2.00 and some cereal boxtops. Its first roll was shot at the High Park Zoo in west Toronto. In 1953 I met Merlin (Moe) Reddy, who always had some oddball camera or other, each a bit more intricate than the last—a three-speed Permaflex, a 2¹/₄ single-lens reflex, a small folding Zeiss 120, etc. Armed with these we made many a trip in Moe's '54 Ford to Toronto's Malton airport. There we experimented in shooting airplanes. We were not very good at it to start.

At Malton I met a few other lads who were keen on airplanes, and some of us started to hitchhike around to airports in southern Ontario. As one fellow would upgrade his camera, I would sometimes inherit the hand-me-down—my first 35mm was Nick Wolochatiuk's old Kodak Pony. It worked fine. Then came Paul Regan's discarded Minolta SR1, my first SLR. The 35s supplemented a trusty Minolta Autocord 2¹/₄ 120 twin-lens reflex used mainly with black and white film. The collection of 3000 negatives that resulted from Autocord days became the catalyst for my first book, *Aviation in Canada*. McGraw-Hill Ryerson published it in 1979, and it enjoyed five printings.

There is a "traditional" way to photograph an airplane. To many over the decades, this supposedly ideal shot has been a 3/4 front angle. The airplane must be static, completely in the clear (no people or vehicles around it, no doors open, stark background, etc.) and in full bright sun. Thirty years ago we would think nothing of waiting for an hour for some mechanics to stop working on an airplane, button it up and go away before we would take our pictures. We were spellbound by the deadly dull airplane photo! In this way, countless excellent photos were passed by as not worthy of attention—aircraft being serviced, dismantled, put back together, being loaded, towed, refuelled, etc.

Little by little, some of us learned that the "people" side of aviation was at least as interesting as the airplanes. Airport buildings and service vehicles even earned their place in our pictures. Thus, instead of waiting for the engine mechanics to go away, we would leave them in our pictures—heresy to most of the photo buffs. We also learned that there was more to lighting than full sun pouring onto the side of an airplane. Excellent photos could be taken on a cloudy day, or even if it was pitch dark (and one had a tripod). Photographing in downpours or in blizzards also paid off. So did shooting aircraft that were taxiing, landing or taking off. All this took a lot more time, energy and imagination than did shooting those static photos, but it was much more fun. We realized that the 3/4 front stock photo was one example of a tradition we didn't need.

In the mid-fifties I finally got airborne. The first flights were with the Air Cadets. Then, by hanging around Toronto Island Airport, I learned a bit about scrounging rides and one week struck it rich with Joe Reed of Airgo. He wanted some air-to-air photos of his fleet. For the fun of the flights, with a few extra circuits in a Luscombe thrown in, Joe got his photos and I my first air-to-airs. One thing led to another, especially at CNE airshow time each year in Toronto. Many a flight was provided by de Havilland, where pilots Bob Fowler, George Neal, Mick Saunders and others got used to our calls scrounging for airshow rides. They easily could have turned us down, but instead found a seat for us in the Otter, Caribou or whichever plane was being demonstrated. In the same period, RCAF public affairs men S/L Dick Bowdery and S/L Bev Totman would have a few of us along on CNE airshow media rides. Thus came the first flights in such types as the Argus, Cosmo, Labrador and Tracker.

Along the way we lads were also fortunate to meet some of the "originals" at the aircraft photo game. We had a certain awe for them—Jack McNulty, Al Martin, Ken Molson, Harvey Stone. They usually worked with old-time cameras such as the 620 Kodak and their methods seemed odd to us.

A real sight was Al Martin and his Speed Graphic! In time we realized what craftsmen these pioneers were and we certainly learned a trick or two from them.

From the late 1950s, some of us would submit our choice photos to aviation magazines. *Air Pictorial* was our favorite and to see our photos in print with a credit was the greatest of fun. Submitting photos gradually led to doing short news stories. Eventually I managed to get the occasional feature story into print through veteran aviation editors Bob Halford and Hugh Whittington (*Aircraft* and *Canadian Aviation* magazines). This led to more opportunities covering the air force and my first flights in fighters and jet trainers. Each flight broadened my experience in shooting air-to-air and built up the photo files. Along the way, many good contacts and associations were made with Air Force personnel at the squadron, base, group and HQ levels. One book began to follow the next and, before I knew it, I was able to walk away from a career in teaching to one as a full-time author and publisher.

While publishing has proven an enjoyable, stimulating profession, the photography side remains the most fun of all. With the ever-changing aviation scene, there seems no danger of running out of material to cover. Throughout the book some of the fundamental techniques of photographing airplanes are mentioned in the captions. Please refer to the Glossary for help with acronyms, etc.

Acknowledgements

The usual thanks are in order to all those who assisted in this project. Many base and squadron commanders were supportive over the years, as were plenty of others from techs on the hangar floor to crews on the flight deck at FL350 or wherever. Some more directly involved include: AIRCOM HQ, BGen Barry Bowen, Molly Brass, CIAS, Ralph Clint, BGen L.W.F. Cuppens. Jerry Davidson, LCol Dan Dempsey, BGen Gordon Diamond, Hank Dielwart, Bud Granley, BGen Fraser Holman, LGen David Huddleston, IMP Aerospace, WO Vic Johnson, Bill Lamberton, LCol R. Levasseur, LCol Dave Lowdon, Col Jack McGee, John McQuarrie, Capt John Moore, Capt Hank Newiadomski, MGen J.D. O'Blenis, LCol Bob Patrick, Capt Don Pearsons, Capt Greg Penner, QIAS, Snowbirds, LGen Fred Sutherland, Ken Swartz, Maj Denis Tabernor, Col Doug Wilson, Capt Ross Wuerth. The names of many others who helped appear in the photo captions.

Larry Milberry

HORNETS

Facing: A 433 Squadron Hornet thunders off the runway at Bagotville, April 19, 1990. Note the various fuel tank configurations on these two pages. Panning a fast-moving target is basic to aircraft photography.

Facing: Hornets 940 and 792 ("416 Golds") join up with their 437 Squadron tanker over northern Alberta on April 3, 1989. As with any other aircraft, misfortune has occasionally befallen the Hornet, but the accident rate is low for the fleet hours recorded by its various operators. 792 crashed on the weapons range at Cold Lake on April 4, 1990. Capt Pierre Trottier lost his life in this unexplained tragedy.

Fighter Group was formed in 1982 just as Canada was to re-equip with the McDonnell Douglas CF-18 Hornet. The new organization had its roots in the RCAF's postwar Air Defence Command and No. 1 Canadian Air Division with their Vampires, CF-100s, F-86s, CF-101s, and CF-104s. Many of Fighter Group's people hailed from those earlier years, assuring a solid foundation as the Hornet began taking over from the last of the fifties generation fighters. To date the Hornet has lived up, not just to the claims made earlier in the flashy sales brochures, but to AIRCOM'S strict standards. Hornet pilots have nothing but praise for their jets. In this April 4, 1989 photo, a CF-18 "dual" of 416 Squadron takes on fuel near Cold Lake as another pilot waits his turn.

The Northrop "CF-18L" prototype at Trenton on September 29, 1978. In fact, this was one of the two YF-17s built to compete in a 1971 USAF requirement for a light weight fighter (LWF). The first YF-17 flew on June 9, 1974, but the following January the Department of Defence chose the General Dynamics F-16 for its LWF. Northrop refocused its sales campaign on NATO and the US Navy. It pursued the USN requirement and joined forces with McDonnell Douglas which had great experience with carrier fighters. In May 1975, the re-designed YF-17 was picked by the Navy and re-designated F/A-18. The much larger F/A-18 made its initial flight on November 18, 1978 and the first squadron (VFA-125) stood up in November 1980. The first CF-18 was rolled out at St. Louis on July 28, 1982; the first CF squadron (410) became operational at Cold Lake in September 1983. The "CF-18L" is now part of the collection at the US Navy Aviation Museum in Pensacola, Florida.

Hornets of 425 Squadron on the ramp at Bagotville April 18, 1990. All six are firing up for an afternoon mission. In the background is the specialized Hornet maintenance hangar.

A lightly configured Hornet takes off at Bagotville on a Fighter Meet 90 sortie. The Hornet gets all the takeoff power it needs from its two General Electric F404-GE-400s of 10,700 lb basic thrust, or 16,000 lb in afterburner. The first RCAF jet fighter, the Vampire, had about one-tenth the thrust.

Above: Hornets of 425 Squadron during refuelling at Bagotville on April 20, 1990.

The refuellers get to work with 790 during FM89.

Top left: Capt Pierre "Mo Mo" Morissette climbs from his Hornet after a Fighter Meet 89 sortie. He will immediately put on his "chem" suit on the tarmac. Such NBCW drills are routinely carried out in all CF units, land, sea or air.

Above: Capt Alain "Alien" Rioux of 433 Squadron returns from a Fighter Meet 89 sortie. An NBCW alert is underway and the groundcrew have Alien's chem suit and gas mask ready for him to don.

Left: Maj Yvan Blondin of 433 is helped into his chem suit following his morning mission of April 13, 1989. Using a telephoto lens lets the photographer keep out of the way but still get "close in" for his shots.

Capts Dan McWilliams and Geoff Boyd of 433 Squadron discuss the tactics from their just-finished FM90 mission. Dan later served with Canadian HQ in Bahrain and Geoff was posted to 419 as an IP.

Below: The formidable Hornet. First delivered to Canada in October 1982, the Hornet has developed into one of the best multirole fighters. Orders totalled 1256 by early 1991. The Hornet can fly at M1.8. It grosses out at 56,000 lb and can lug up to 17,000 lb of external stores. Length is 56', wing span 37'6" and height 15'4". Wing area is a mere 400 sq ft. This view shows the handsome lines of the Hornet in plan view.

Left: Col Fraser Holman, base commander at Bagotville at the time, prepares for an FM90 Hornet trip, April 19, 1990. He was later promoted and posted to NATO HQ.

Right: Maj Carl Dahlin and Capt Herb Dannenberg of the 148th FIG (Minnesota ANG) sign paperwork for their F-4D Phantom following an FM90 sortie. Such meets are invaluable training opportunities. Things get wild on any one of the morning or afternoon "wars". Fighters are bombing or defending targets, "getting tapped", they're up high and down low, on the "initial push" in to a target, regrouping, etc. At a debrief all the fighter jargon can be heard... "Try to tire out your enemy, make him turn and burn when he's going home low on gas... let's hear your kill acknowledgement... those A-10s are flying too damn low and slow for me to see... those ain't A-10s, they're fast snowmobiles... go for max allowable risk... the Hornets will sanitize the area... the 'comm' goes down hill as the battle evolves... couldn't ask for any better GCI...."

Below: Also at FM90 were the F-4s of VMFA-321, the US Marine Corps reserve unit from Andrews AFB, DC. By 1995 the F-4 will have pretty well faded from US military service.

Facing page: A 425 Hornet at Bagotville where a mobile repair team from a civilian contractor was carrying out a vital spar mod. In the second photo, techs tow 786 from its hangar at Bagotville on April 12, 1989. The famous 433 porcupine symbol is on the tail and the hangar wall.

A pair of A-10 Warthogs (103rd TFG, Connecticut ANG) gets up for an FM90 sortie. Each carries an AIM-9 "Lima" AAM for self defence. At FM90 the A-10s were violated once for attacking low flying (200' AGL) intruders from *below!* Some jealous fast jet driver was heard at debrief to whine, "These A-10 guys have been acting big lately." In the Gulf War the A-10 was outstanding, contrary to all the nay-sayers who predicted its demise in combat.

Typical scene at another Canada-US fighter meet, this one at Burlington, Vermont sponsored in May 1989 by the 158th FIG. The meet was "Maple Leaf" and included the F-16, F/A-18C, CF-18, F-14, F-4, A-4 and E-2. Here two 433 CF-18s sit between an F/A-18C and an F-16A.

Canada's 1988 pilot team at the William Tell air weapons meet at Tyndall AFB, Florida. They were from 441 Squadron at Cold Lake: Maj Stu Holdsworth, Capts Hollis Tucker, Dave Burton and René Leblanc, and Maj Bob Wade. The rest of the team comprised groundcrew and air weapons controller. The competition was mainly F-15s from various USAF squadrons. Willy Tell 90 was cancelled due to the Persian Gulf crisis (or, as the fighter jocks say, it was re-located to Iraq!).

Capts Hollis Tucker and Guy Sawchuck during off-hours at Willy Tell 88. Hollis lost his life on April 22, 1990 while on a mission from the 441 Det at Comox. His Hornet (188772) inexplicably dove into the sea from high altitude.

The 441 team starts engines for an early morning Willy Tell 88 sortie over the Gulf of Mexico. By getting up early, the photographer can capture the soft light at daybreak.

The groundcrew tow 416 Hornet No. 798 to the flightline at Cold Lake. The wingtips had been folded for hangar storage (a handy feature inherited from the naval F/A-18). This photo shows that backlighting has a value of its own.

Juxtaposed types. Hornet 706 at Trenton for the QIAS on June 22, 1990 as a 424 "Lab" charges off.

In the twilight over Northern Alberta, two 416 jets fade to silhouettes. Others, the light now too low for hand-held Kodachrome 64, jump around on the film.

A two-seat Hornet of 416 Squadron takes on fuel during the AR exercise at Cold Lake April 4, 1989.

TACTICAL AIR MEET

A typical scene at Baden, home of Tactical Air Meet '88, a big NATO fighter meet. Note how dirty aircraft get in the industrially polluted Rhine Valley environment. Canada's Hornets have been serving at CFB Baden-Soellingen since 1985 when 409 Squadron arrived from Cold Lake. 421 and 439 joined it in the following months. The three squadrons constituted No. 1 Canadian Air Division, part of Canadian Forces Europe. 409 led Canada's air contingent into the Persian Gulf in October 1990. In March 1991 Ottawa announced that 409 would be disbanded as part of the gradual reduction of Canada's NATO forces in view of rapidly evolving European conditions.

At 409 Squadron servicing, July 22, 1988. WO Jerry Gares discusses technical details as LCol Dave Bartram (CO, 409) and Capt Dave "Stinger" Anderson get ready to walk to their jets for a TAM '88 sortie from Baden.

TAM 88 partners seen at Baden on July 21: an F.3 Tornado from 29 Squadron, RAF Coningsby lands; Mirage 2000s of 2nd FW, Dijon-Longvic wait on the ramp; an F-16 of the 52nd TFW, (Spangdahlen) on its takeoff roll; and an F-104S of Italy's 9th Wing lands. A midsize zoom lens is ideal for photos like these.

A GR1 Tornado of 617 "The Dam Busters" Squadron from RAF Marham. Such a photo captures some of the hustle and bustle of a busy meet.

Left: July 21 was media day at TAM 88. Dozens of tail number "nuts", were given their hour of glory to jot down numbers and burn up the film. Here they line the main runway at Baden. The Europeans lead the world in this frantic hobby. Toronto photographer Ken Swartz is in the foreground ready to shoot departing fighters.

A new angle on the 439 Squadron four-ship flown from Baden on March 13, 1987 (the original ones were published in *Canada's Air Force Today*). Such a view is an aircraft photographer's dream – sitting in the spacious Hornet shooting merrily away. Leading is Capt Ken Gerhards in 188740. Left wing in 769 is Capt Kirk Leuty, right is Capt Chris Grasswick in 761. The photo ship was 919 flown by Maj Ray Levasseur. A few weeks later (May 4) Capt Gerhards and Capt Dean Beselt punched out of 919 south of Baden when it "departed controlled flight". 761 crashed at RAF Alconbury on October 20, 1987 when there was trouble on take off. Capt Dean Freidt found his machine unwilling to rotate, got a flight control systems caution light and aborted takeoff. As 761 aquaplaned on the runway, Freidt ejected at 100 KIAS. 761 rolled up into a ball, the fuselage crushing the cockpit. Freidt nearly landed on the wreckage. He had no serious injuries. Capt Leuty was killed in a midair collision on April 17, 1990 over Karlsruhe, Germany between 765 (Leuty) and 779 (Capt Reg Decoste). Gerhards and Grasswick later joined the airlines while Levasseur became CO of 433 Squadron.

"Red Indian" (421 Squadron) pilots, Lee "Lob" Obst and Bob "Cowboy" Pinchaud return with all their gear from a TAM88 mission, July 21, 1988.

THE GULF WAR

Shortly after Iraq invaded Kuwait on August 2, 1990, Canada joined a US-led United Nations movement to oust Iraqi forces from their new "province". On August 10 Canada agreed to send a three-ship flotilla to patrol the Persian Gulf and help enforce an embargo against Iraq. On September 14 it announced that CF-18s would be going to Qatar to strengthen UN forces. The first of 18 CF-18s (primarily of 409 Squadron, bolstered by other units) flew from Baden to Doha, Qatar on October 6. Later, 409 was replaced by 439 augmented mainly by 416. The "Persian Excursion" Hornets (eventually numbering 26) were a fully operational force. Typical is this one on the "hot" flightline at Doha. It carries AIM-9 Sidewinder AAMs on the wingtips and two pairs of AIM-7 Sparrows. The M61 six-barrel 20mm cannon in the nose is armed, and all-up fuel is carried, including three external tanks.

Groundcrew and pilot busy in the pre-flight phase of an upcoming CAP from Doha.

Capt Emile Calderon does pre-flight paperwork on January 14, 1991. Two of his crewmen, Cpls Allen Robinson and Serge Faucher, look on. Then, Calderon ready to taxi. He logged 21 missions during the war and returned to Canada on March 11 to a hero's welcome.

On January 16, 1991 Canada went to war for the first time since the Korean conflict (1950–1953). On the 24th, CF-18s flew their first missions over Iraq. Here 769 awaits some action at Doha as 437 tanker No. 704 comes in to land following a mission over Saudi Arabia.

Capts Emile Calderon and Rob Cox turn away from the racket and jet blast as Hornets taxi out for a sortie.

Facing: Capt Rob Cox, one of Canada's "Desert Cats", lounges by his jet, waiting for a CAP mission to launch.

Above: Groundcrew await the return of four CF-18s at Doha on January 14. Beyond are Qatari hardened aircraft shelters appropriately camouflaged. CF-18s at Doha flew some 2700 missions including about 40 air-to-ground trips in the last few days of the war (which ended on February 28).

Desert Cats groundcrew, those indispensable "cogs in the wheel" stand by to service arriving Hornets. Any broad-based aviation book will give plenty of space to the people who fly and support the airplanes.

Easy does it—groundcrew relax in warm Qatari sunshine, waiting for action at Doha. It was never long in coming.

Capt Doug "Dog" Carter just down from an afternoon
CAP. He carries his kit across the ramp to catch the
minibus back to Ops. The refuellers begin readying the
jets for immediate turnaround. During the war, the CF-18s
did not fire on any Iraqi fighters in combat—the Iraqi airforce was mostly kept in HASs or had fled to Iran.

Pilots back from a CAP over the Persian Gulf on January 14 head to Ops for debrief.

Armourers download an AIM-7 at Doha. Driving is Cpl Robert Williams. Left is Cpl Joe Verreault, then MCpl Steve Szabo.

All the starboard nose details for the IPMS gang appear in this view of 188746 as it sits at Doha. The "false canopy", painted in black, is visible on the underside. It is there to help confuse the enemy during combat.

Fighter pilots are regular guys too! Capt Jeff Beckett and Maj Van "Poncho" Peterson wash up their dishes in the mess at Canada Dry 2, their camp at Doha.

Views at Doha of two more Hornets—752 ready to go, 758 just back from an afternoon CAP. Both bristle with missiles. During the war, only once was a Canadian missile fired—on January 29, Maj Dave Kendall fired an AIM-7 at an Iraqi patrol boat, but did not find the target. Of 39 American air-to-air kills during the war, 25 were made by AIM-7s.

THE CF-5

The Northrop CF-5 is Canada's advanced fighter trainer, serving with 419 "Moose" Squadron. It was built by Canadair (135 for CF) and entered service in 1968 with 434 Squadron at Cold Lake. It later served with "four tree tree" Porcépic Squadron at Bagotville. CF-5 116703 bears a festive paint scheme commemorating the Moose Squadron's illustrious history. Three Harvards trail smoke overhead in this QIAS 90 shot. Simple timing assured the desired composition.

Maj Tom Manderson and Capt Reimer Kujala (419 Squadron IPs) in CF-5s 717 and 750 en route Trenton–Cold Lake on April 3, 1989.

CANADA'S FIRST JET FIGHTER

The RCAF's first operational jet was the de Havilland Vampire (1948–1956). With a top speed of about 550 mph, the "Vamp" was a great little toy for the fighter jocks. The RCAF had 86, used mainly by the air reserve, as well as the fighter OTU at St. Hubert and Chatham, and 410 Squadron (which formed Canada's first jet aerobatic team in 1949). In 1956 the air reserve got Sabre 5s and the Vamps were sold. Many went to the Mexican Air Force via a US agent. N6875D is seen at Malton in November 1959. It was one of a flock

of Vampires that had been weathering at Malton for some time. Suddenly, they were towed out of the weeds, dusted off, fired up and flown away—no problem!

The Vampire was Britain's second jet fighter design (next to the Meteor). It was first flown on September 20, 1943. The RCAF flew trials with a Vampire F.1 in 1946 and formed its first squadron (410) with F.3s in December 1948.More than three decades later only two remain airworthy. N41J (ex RCAF 17031) was restored over an eight year period by United Airlines Capt Bill Lamberton, and is shown during Bill's visit to Comox April 17-18, 1991. N41J is the world's oldest flying jet. It was originally assembled in Toronto and made its first flight in April 1947.

Bill Lamberton banks and dives gently while easily holding formation with a 442 Squadron Buffalo at about 130 KIAS. In the photo below, the Vampire nudges in behind the 442 Squadron Buffalo. For its time, the Vampire was a reasonable fighter, having a top speed of 400+ knots. It was manoeuvrable, had a ceiling of more than 40,000' and was armed with 4 x 20mm cannons.

N41J—no prettier jet fighter, with such clean, unpretentious lines. This example flew for some years with Al Hansen of Mojave, California. Bill Lamberton purchased it in 1982, flew it a little, then began restoration. In its "born again" form it first flew on April 12, 1991. One drawback with this type (as far as longevity goes) has been its plywood and balsa fuselage.

The Vampire showing its 442 Squadron markings (SL code). Behind the canopy is its only non-period feature—a modern communication antenna. This F.3 cruises at around 300 KIAS. Internal fuel is 330 Imp. gal. but two 100 Imp. gal. underwing tanks are optional.

N41J, engine inspection doors open, sits at Comox shortly after arriving on April 17. Its 3000-lb thrust Goblin engine smoked for several minutes in traditional fashion (to the astonishment of the onlookers).

Right: Col Jack McGee, Comox base commander and longtime naval aviator, chats with Bill Lamberton. Bill had joined the RCAF auxiliary in 1956, flying T-33s, Harvards and Expeditors with 443 "City of New Westminster" Squadron. In 1959 he joined Transair, moved to Pacific Western Airlines, then United in 1964. It had long been his dream to fly his own jet. His Vampire may not impress a young Hornet pilot too much, but Bill loves it!

Close-up of the neatly shaped "Vamp". Total airframe hours on 17031/ N41J on April 18, 1991 was 1462, nearly all with the RCAF.

Right: Airmen gather 'round the Vampire as the Snowbirds practice overhead. The Vampire is roughly comparable to a Tutor: wing span 40' (Tutor, 36'6"), length 30'9" (32'), wing area 262 sq. ft. (220), gross weight 12,000 lb (7,800), thrust 3100 lb (2950), speed 450-500 mph.

Above: 442 Squadron had formed with the Spitfire Vb February 1944. It disbanded August 1945, then re-formed April 1946 in Vancouver. It flew Vampires April 1948–October 1956 when the Sabre 5 took over. It again disbanded, but was reconstituted in July 1968. Here N41J sits in waning light with a 442 Buffalo. Evening light has its own special qualities.

Vampire 17074 belongs to the National Aviation Museum, and also carries the 442 code letters.

THE CLUNK

A first class aircraft of its category and vintage, the Avro CF-100 exemplified the best in Canadian know-how during the postwar years. It showed what the country could do and rightfully became a nationalistic symbol. It combined Canadian airframe and engine design with the Hughes airborne intercept fire control system from the US. The result was the world's finest all-weather interceptor at a time when the threat of Soviet bomber attack on the West was as real as it was ever going to be. 692 CF-100s were completed from 1949 - 1958 (first flight was January 19, 1950). This example, a Mark 5 on loan to Avro, was landing on Runway 32 at Malton on July 6, 1960. The CF-100 was succeeded at Avro by the mighty CF-105 Arrow. It, however, was scrapped by Ottawa in 1959 while still under development. The Arrow never got to prove itself one way or the other beyond the flight test program. Its fate is still much bemoaned by those who worked on the project, and the Avro Arrow "cult following" that has arisen over the years.

Above: This CF-100 MK.4B was shot on July 8, 1960 as it taxied by the photographer's favorite spot at Malton at the time—beside the Sanderson-Acfield sales office. 18478 wore the yellow and black colours of 432 Squadron from Bagotville.

Stripped-out EW CF-100s in the scrap heap at CFB Trenton (Mountain View Det.) in June 1991.

Often referred to as the "Clunk", the CF-100 served until late 1981. At first it had equipped NORAD and NATO all-weather fighter squadrons, and in a second career was an electronic warfare trainer for NORAD with the EW Unit at St. Hubert, then with 414 (EW) Squadron in Ottawa and North Bay. Clunk 100784 is over Northern Ontario on January 4, 1980, shot from a 414 Falcon.

Over the years it has been fun tracking individual airplane histories. Here is the same CF-100 on display at CFB Baden-Soellingen. It was flown there on December 17, 1981—the last of countless trans-Atlantic Clunks. Capts Bud Milne and Pete Maunsell of 414 made the delivery.

CANADAIR SABRE

Above: The most famed postwar RCAF fighter was the Canadair-built F-86 Sabre. 1184 were on strength 1950–1970. Sabres epitomized the RCAF's postwar glory days. Many have been preserved for posterity, this one at CFB Lahr. It commemorates 444 Squadron's Sabre days in Germany from September 1953 to February 1963. This is actually an ex-Luftwaffe Sabre.

The prototype Canadair Sabre is displayed at CFB Edmonton bearing the PX code of CEPE. Beyond is a T-33 in 408 markings, and a Bomarc to honour 447 (SAM) Squadron (which later flew Chinooks as 447 TACHEL Squadron from Edmonton).

101s & 104s

When Canada abandoned the Avro Arrow, it replaced it with a combination of CF-101 Voodoo interceptors and Bomarc "B" surface-to-air missiles. This system worked successfully within NORAD for many years. The Voodoo was the ultimate refinement of a 1946 McDonnell design, the XF-88. The first Voodoo flew in October 1954, the first RCAF examples arrived in Edmonton in October 1961, and the last did not leave service until early 1987. 17450 was shot at Trenton on August 30, 1962—a majestic-looking aircraft, even on the ground. 17450 was later traded back to the USAF for a more current model. It went to the Nevada ANG and in 1975 flew to the USAF boneyard at Davis-Monthan AFB, Arizona.

This CF-101 was one of the last two of its type in AIRCOM service. It was the so-called "Electric Voodoo" used in EW training with 414 Squadron. It's seen on April 4, 1987 from a 414 T-33.

Old Voodoos in "the boonies" at Bagotville on April 12, 1989. 425 Squadron's "Lark One" is first in line. In the distance are the NORAD alert hangars from CF-100 days. Two UH-1 Huey hulks are on the right. By 1991 most AIRCOM Voodoos were still around, mainly as ABDR resources, but quite a few also have museum or gate guardian status.

Right: Soviet Bear "kill" symbol on boneyard Voodoo 882B at Mountain View in 1991.

The sleek Canadair-built Lockheed CF-104 Starfighter replaced the Sabre in Canadian NATO Squadrons. It served 1963 - 1986 and is remembered by those who flew it as an outstanding fighter. Although many pilots lost their lives on "104" missions, the airplane was almost never at fault. These three of 417 Squadron were shot at Abbotsford on August 13, 1976. A vantage point above ground level enhances such a lineup shot—in this case the wing of a C-130.

EXOTIC VISITORS

Each year there are many "hands-across-the-border" events with CF and US
military aircraft visiting each other's bases for exercises or air shows. Here is
part of the scene at the 1990 QIAS at CFB Trenton. This is one of Canada's
leading airshows and, weather permitting, draws a huge crowd. A hangar
roof was the vantage point here.

The Rockwell B-1B visited Trenton for the first time in June 1990.

The B-1B, awesome in shape and colour, casts its shadow on the tarmac at Trenton. Three vintage RCAF jets are dwarfed by the bomber in this early morning view from Hank Dielwart's Chipmunk.

The first appearance of the modern Soviet Air Force in North America occurred at the 1989 Abbotsford International Air Show. In 1990 two MiG-29s visited Canada and the US, their first official show being in Ottawa at the National Capital Air Show. Here the MiGs arrive (June 18) from Winnipeg. LCol "Louie" Levasseur, CO of 433 Squadron, leads the formation with Capt Moe Girard in the slot. Left wing is MiG pilot Valerie Minitsky, right wing is Roman Taskaev.

Roman (left) and Valerie (right) just after climbing from their MiGs at Ottawa. Centre is Yuri Bramkov who was in the back seat of Valerie's MiG.

Below: The MiG-29s pull up to the ramp at Ottawa. With today's range of films, a decent exposure can be gotten on any dull day.

Facing page: A real national symbol, Canada's ever-popular Snowbirds celebrated 20 years of flying in 1990. They annually represent Canada's armed forces at air displays throughout North America. Five of the nine-plane team are shown over Howe Sound on the British Columbia coast on April 5, 1990. In this formation (from the bottom) are Brooke Lawrence, Steve Will, Dan Dempsey (Lead), Ross Granley and Dale Hackett.

THE SNOWBIRDS

Ancestors of the Snowbirds were the Golden Centennaires who did airshows in 1967 celebrating Canada's 100th birthday. CO of the team was W/C O.B. Philp, with S/L C.B. Lang as team lead. Here Tutor 153 was at Mount Hope, Ontario for an airshow May 13, 1967. In 1991 it was an instructional airframe at the School of Aerospace Technology and Engineering at CFB Borden.

26151 was one of the original Snowbirds aircraft. It flew in the CIAS in Toronto on September 5, 1970 and was shot that day at Downsview.

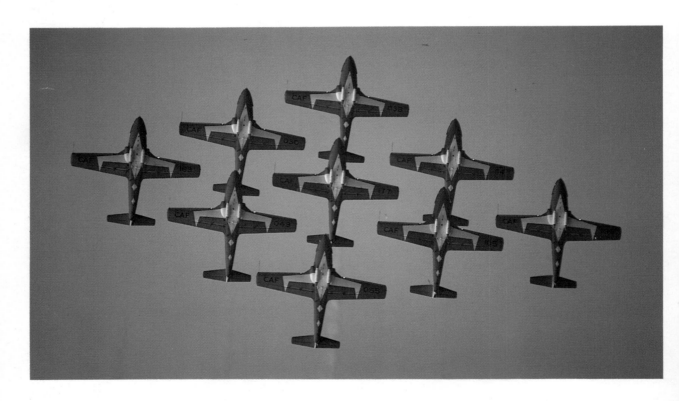

Above: The 1983 Snowbirds perform in Toronto on the Labour Day Weekend. Lead (in 114036) is Maj George Hawey in this view of the famous Big Diamond formation. No. 2 (114114) is Capt Geoff Gamble, No. 3 (114030)—Capt Bill Ryan, No. 4 (114177)—Capt Tristan deKoninck, No. 5 (114055)—Capt Holmes Patton, No. 6 (114105)—Capt Richie Clements, No. 7 (114049)—Capt Rob Chapman, No. 8 (114190)—Capt Bob Stephan, No. 9 (114163)—Capt Jon Graham. deKoninck died in a CF-18 crash near CFB Summerside on May 24, 1986. Stephan became team leader in 1991.

9
7   3
  5   4   1
6   2
  8

Above: The 1990 Snowbirds at Comox on April 5 in Concorde formation: No. 1 Maj Dan Dempsey, No. 2 Capt Ross Granley, No. 3 Capt Steve Will, No. 4 Capt Vincent Jandrisch, No. 5 Capt John Low, No. 6 Capt Dale Hackett, No. 7 Capt Brooke Lawrence, No. 8 Capt Les Racicot, No. 9 Capt Rich Lancaster.

The 1991 team in Wedge formation.

Diving through with the Concorde. The Snowbirds first used this formation in 1977, looped it the following year, and rolled it in 1986.

The Snowbirds roll seemingly this way and that as they execute their flashy 1990 Philion manoeuvre. It was named in honour of Joey Philion, a resilient teen from Orillia, Ontario severely burned in a house fire.

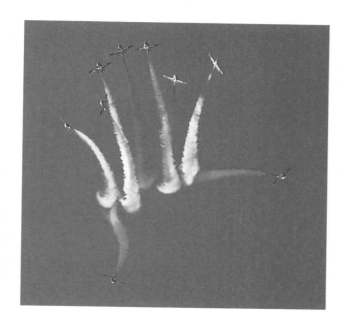

Downward Bomb Burst—best viewed looking straight up!

Big Diamond at Comox in 1990 with Snowbird chase carrying ex-RCAF Sabre pilot (now film maker) Bob Gibson. This formation readily transforms into Concorde.

The seven-plane Maple Burst, Comox, 1990.

The team co-ordinator's Tutor sits idle at Comox as a Snowbird seven-plane approaches, 1990.

Above: Les Racicot, Rich Lancaster, Dale Hackett, John Low and Brooke Lawrence back from a practice session during "spring training camp" at Comox in April 1990.

Below: Ross Granley (No. 2) and his sister, Stacey, at the National Capital Air Show, June 29, 1990. Several in the Granley family are fliers. Ross' father, Bud, flies 747-400s for United Airlines (he had flown Sabres in the RCAF), and his brother Chris flies CF-18s (having done a USAF tour on F-16s).

Above: The 1990 team relaxes in the morning sun at Comox: Ross Granley, Ross Fetterly (admin. officer), Jeff Hill (commentator), Dale Hackett and Brooke Lawrence (autographing).

Cpl Tony Edmundson, Snowbirds aero-engine tech, did secondary duty in 1991 as show video tech. Tony joined the service in 1984 after graduating from the Southern Alberta Institute of Technology. He earned both private pilot and air maintenance engineer licences and worked several years on Tutors before joining the team.

More easy goin' at Comox. Dom Taillon and Tony Edmundson standing on the left. Around the card table are Brooke Lawrence, Vinny Jandrisch, Steve Will, Dale Hackett and John Low. Right are Ross Granley and Mario Deshaies.

Below: Combining foreground with background. Photographer Rafe Tomsett changes film at Comox as the team hurtles earthward.

Below: Maj Dan Dempsey (1980-81 Solo, 1989-90 Lead) discusses photos with Bill Johnson. Bill and O.B. Philp are authors of *Snowbirds: From the Beginning*, one of the finest aviation books of recent years. Bill, a long-time Seattle resident, is the team's photographer emeritus.

The team gets airborne for an April 1990 practice session.

The Arrow in silhouette from below over Comox: No. 1 Dan Dempsey, No. 2 Ross Granley, No. 3 Steve Will, No. 4 Vinny Jandrisch, No. 5 John Low, No. 6 Dale Hackett, No. 7 Brooke Lawrence.

Left: Groundcrew manhandle a Tutor at Comox.

Below: The Snowbirds, tailed by the CWH Lancaster, pass over AMDU Road on the west side of CFB Trenton, June 22, 1990. The photo was taken by hanging out the side of Capt Hank Dielwart's Chipmunk. Hank, an EWO at the time with 414 Squadron, is an avid sport aviator.

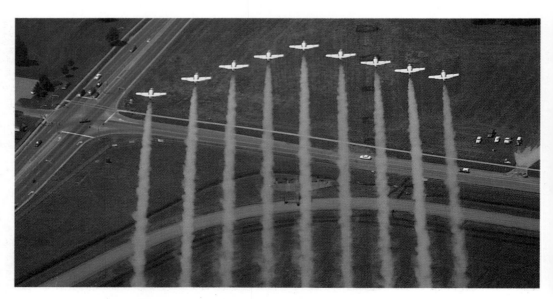

Over "the Rocks" north of Comox, in April 1990 the Snowbirds roll. Vinny Jandrisch is straight ahead, seen from Snowbird 5 (John Low). This is life on the edge!

Maj Dan Dempsey leads the team onto the ramp at Comox following a practice session on April 6, 1990.

Dale Hackett, Les Racicot and Dominic Taillon (team co-ordinator) over BC's coastal mountains. The Tutor is a good photo plane—lots of elbow room and little problem with canopy reflection.

The entire team in flight off Comox in April 1990. In the photo below, Dale Hackett, 1990 "Snowbird 6", flies level as Les Racicot, "Snowbird 8", banks away. One takes many such photos to get one good enough to publish.

Two views in contrasting light of Snowbird Tutors at Comox, April 17, 1991. Below, the team is flashing up for a photo mission. Commentator Jeff Hill is in the foreground.

Early morning at Comox during the team's 1991 training session.

Looking down the line—11 Tutors. The Boss' jet is No. 1, Nos. 2-9 are show planes, No. 10 is chase and No. 11 is a utility jet that carries a tool and spares kit in the right seat. Enticing subject, light and background.

Some of the local Comox Valley school kids get the morning off to watch the 1991 Snowbirds practice.

Following a photo flight on April 17, 1991 the gang poses on the ramp at Comox. In front are Brooke Lawrence, Ross Granley, Bill Watts, Rich Lancaster and Glenn Oerzen. Behind are Bob Stephan (Lead), Vinny Jandrisch, "civy" photographers Tony Gasbarro, Rick Radell, Jerry Davidson, John McQuarrie and Rafe Tomsett, Réal Turgeron, Marc Robert and Nick Cassidy.

Maj Bob Stephan, 1991 Lead, autographs programs for Snowbirds fans. Bob took over from Dan Dempsey who was posted to AIRCOM HQ at the end of the 1990 season. Bob's background is mainly CF-5s. He filled a Snowbirds solo slot in 1983-84 and in 1989.

Yogi Huyghebaert and team supply tech, Darcy Gallipeau, strap into a Tutor following a visit to Comox from Moose Jaw in April 1991. Yogi flew solo with the team in 1974-75, then Lead 1985-86. Each Lead has contributed something unique to the team's evolution, be it tangible, such as a new or modified manoeuvre, or (just as important) intangible, such as the mark he makes on team attitude and spirit.

In the late 1950s, the RCAF's Harvard demo team, the Goldilocks, devised their "crazy" formation. Team leader, Jerry Davidson (seen on facing page) introduced this crowd-pleasing manoeuvre. At the 1991 spring training session, Jerry arranged for this "set up" shot of the crazy formation with Tutors instead of Harvards.

Snowbirds tech at work and play—Cpl Rick Macnab lugs a seatpack and safety equipment from a Tutor into the Snowbirds shack at Comox, then is snapped during lunchbreak practicing his football. A former airforce reservist, Rick joined the "reg force" in 1986 and gained four years experience at Moose Jaw before joining the team in 1990. For such "people shots" a medium telephoto is handiest.

Facing page: VU-33 in Comox (destined to merge with 414 Squadron) today has an all-T-bird fleet (in 1990 it lost its three Trackers to budget cuts). Here 564 and 577 undergo maintenance. Several of AIRCOM's T-birds now have 10,000+ flying hours.

Cpl Marco Asselin, a first year aero-engine tech with the 1991 team, polishes the windscreen on Snowbird 2 flown by Ross Granley. The techs work long hours to keep their birds spotless and mechanically perfect.

Each year the Snowbirds are covered by a group of seasoned photographers. There are the old timers like Bill Johnson, and always a few new boys. Ottawa photographer John McQuarrie started shooting the team in earnest in 1990. He had earlier proved his stuff with his 1990 book *Canadian Wings*. Here he is just back with his feet on the ground after an April 17, 1991 photo flight from Comox.

T-birds of old: the Golden Centennaires' hack at Hamilton on May 13, 1967; and (facing page) , on August 20, 1976, an ex-CF aircraft purchased from Crown Assets and colourfully painted up by its Edmonton owner.

The Lockheed T-33 is one of history's great aviation achievements. Developed from the P-80 Shooting Star (first flown January 8, 1944), it served in many air arms and continues in use. AIRCOM's "T-birds" serve a multitude of roles from target towing, to threat simulation, to EW training. In the photos below, Capt Lou Glussich (with EWO Capt Kevin Hale, USAF) flies 133571 of 414 (EW) Squadron on a mission from CFB Bagotville, April 12, 1989. Note the T-bird's "stealth" colour scheme.

T-bird 352 and stablemates of VU-32 Squadron seen at CFB Shearwater in November 1990. The VU-32 T-birds are kept busy with various fleet support duties. In the far corner is 266, written off after it was overstressed in flight. Note the tit on the nose—an ASQ-503 threat emitter. In 1991 VU-32 was operating six T-33s and had eight pilots. Crowded and dark as they often are, hangars can still offer some good shooting opportunities.

A crowd of 414 Squadron "Black Knights" with their EW detachment at William Tell 88: MCpl Kirk Johnson, Capt Al Sutherland, MCpl Bruce Taylor, MCpl Dan Berthiaume, WO Thompson, Cpl Jacques Huard and Capt Bob Normand. The T-birds were playing "bad guy", so their tiptanks are appropriately decorated.

Facing page: T-bird "triple three" heads the flightline at Bagotville on April 18, 1990. There always seems to be a T-bird around! A Huey was the camera ship.

TRAINING

Musketeer 238 during a photo flight on November 15, 1990. Capt Steve Stuart, an IP with No. 3 CFFTS is flying 238. Cohort, Capt Sylvain Besner, is flying the photo plane (241). The Musketeer, first in CF service in 1971, replaced the Chipmunk as the air force's primary trainer. The original batch of 25 was replaced by 25 new Musketeers in 1981 and now those may have to be replaced if the DND farms out primary fixed wing pilot training to a civil contractor. By then the Musketeer will have trained 1000s of neophyte pilots with very few serious mishaps. One of the last of those occurred March 23, 1990 when 229 had an engine failure on takeoff from Russell, Manitoba (where it had been hopping Air Cadets). The plane force landed without injury, but damage was severe enough that it was later cannibalized.

Capts Besner and Stuart following their photo sortie.

Musketeer 242 of the Primary Flying School "in the barn" at Portage. Basic aircraft maintenance has been done at Portage, but DLIRs have been done for No. 3 FTS by Field Aviation in Calgary (Musketeers) and Bristol Aerospace and Canadian Helicopters (Jet Rangers/Kiowas).

Below: An odd mix of BHS aircraft at Portage on November 15, 1990: two standard BHS Jet Rangers, one in UN colours with da-glo red doors, and two Kiowas borrowed from 10TAG/ Air Reserve to bolster its resources while some Jet Rangers were on loan to the 89th Rotary Wing Aviation Unit in Honduras.

Kiowas (238, 216) in maintenance at Portage in November 1990. When No. 3 FTS/BHS was asked to lend Jet Rangers to the 89th RWAU in 1989, the strain was eased by borrowing Kiowas. As of October 24, 1990 the BHS was operating 10 of each type, its high time Jet Ranger (1981 models) being 139305 (5265 hours) and its high time Kiowa (1971 models) being 136216 (10756.7 hours).

The North American Harvard was the RCAF's advanced trainer for years. The first ones entered service in 1939, the last left in 1965. Many Canadian-built Harvards survive. These ones of the Canadian Harvard Association roared in to CFB Trenton in June 1990 for the Quinte International Air Show. Each is authentically painted, C-FVCJ appearing as 20415 (RCAF dates: October 10, 1952–August 15, 1966). When disposed of in the sixties by Crown Assets, a fly-away Harvard could be purchased for about $2000. Today's market value of one of these glorious old warbirds could be over $100,000.

Below: Prior to going on Harvards, postwar RCAF pilot candidates started on the delightful little Chipmunk. Here 18004 from Centralia taxis on the grass at Kitchener-Waterloo airport in southern Ontario. It was visiting for a Sunday morning breakfast fly-in on July 9, 1961.

Above: Harvard 372, trailing smoke, roars over Trenton on June 1, 1963. This aircraft crashed October 6, 1964.

King Air 200s (CF designation: CT-145) 145201 and 202 at Winnipeg on November 14, 1990. They were leased for a year from Awood Aviation of Thunder Bay in October 1990 to give the ICPS (Instrument Check Pilot School) a multi-engine proficiency trainer following phase out of the Dakota. A five-week, 22-hour course was being offered on the CT-145 in 1991.

For future advanced pilot training, AIRCOM may use a modern turboprop. AIRCOM evaluates options as they come along—the Beech T-34C, Pilatus PC-9, Embraer Tucano, etc. Here is the Brazilian Tucano in flight over Ottawa on June 27, 1990. Test pilot Antonio Bragança Silva was demonstrating it at the National Capital Air Show.

Tutor 086 taxiing to the ramp at RCAF Station Ottawa in June 1965. It's in the standard bare metal finish of the day with red paint on the extremities. This aircraft crashed in December 1971 following engine failure on climbout. The student ejected safely.

Instructor and student climb aboard Tutor 184 at the Flying Instructors School at CFB Portage la Prairie. The FIS annually trains about 72 new instructor pilots, most of whom are "pipeliners" destined for a tour at Moose Jaw. Beyond are Jet Rangers of the Basic Helicopter School.

114042 taxis out for a student-IP trip from No. 2 CFFTS, Moose Jaw, July 10, 1987. The marvellous little Tutor will likely see the turn of the century in CF service. It has trained many pilots over the decades and logged well over 1,000,000 flying hours—the Canadian taxpayer ought to be pleased!

Below: A diminutive Tutor sits alongside two hefty CF-18s at Comox on April 5, 1990.

THE MIGHTY HERC

The backbone of Air Transport Group, and of troop and freight operations in many airforces, is the ubiquitous Lockheed C-130 Hercules. This "Herc" LAPES exercise was at Mountain View on June 8, 1991.

The "loadie" opens the port sliding door. Moments later the 1 Commando boys flung themselves onto Anzio drop zone at CFB Petawawa.

ATG's Hercs are flying trucks for the army. Troops of 1 Commando, Canadian Airborne Regiment, board a Herc at Trenton for parachute training, June 6, 1991.

Workhorse of the airways, DC-3 of the propjet era—the Lockheed C-130 Hercules. First flown on August 23, 1954, the "Herc" entered RCAF service in 1960. Three decades later Canada is still buying Hercs—five C-130H-90s in 1990. All around the world the Herc has proven itself an indispensable transport that can get in and out of marginal strips. Air Transport Group has proven this many times during UN humanitarian operations—in Kurdistan, Ethiopia, Niger, Azerbaidzhan, Namibia, Honduras, etc. This 436 Herc was loading a CF helicopter in Honduras on November 27, 1990 following a UN Central American operation. During the Gulf War, ATG Hercs logged 10,048 hours on ops. This was ATG's largest-ever airlift.

Life aboard a 436 Squadron Herc. Flight engineer Sgt Dan Daniels gets ready to enjoy his hot meal prepared by loadmaster MCpl Rob Sowatsky. The Herc is 130325 (UN Flt. 6532) operating Trenton-Tegucigalpa with cargo for the 89th RWAU November 27-28, 1990. Capt Mike Allen, the AC, is in the background. The FO was his "big boss", BGen Gord Diamond.

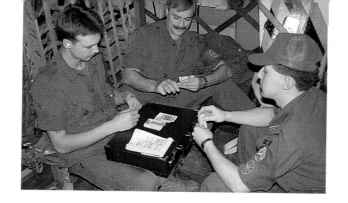

In the back end of 325, three of the troops from Trenton's mobile air movements section (MAMS) pass the time away playing cards—Cpl Rick Barrett, Cpl Dan Brinklow and Pte Dave Baker. They were heading to Tegucigalpa to load a Twin Huey for Fredericton.

Beautiful but aviators beware—ominous "CBs" (cumulonimbus) over Florida as 325 heads north.

Late night at Fredericton, and techs from 403 Squadron (CFB Gagetown) shoehorn Twin Huey 112 from the Herc.

Below: 130325 on the ramp at Fredericton, November 29, 1990. Air Transport Group's motto is "Versatile and Ready", 436's is "*Onus Portamus*—We Carry the Load". So they are, and so they do. For such exposures a tripod is best. In this case the fender of a truck had to suffice.

The original RCAF C-130E was 10305. The "E"s were acquired in 1965 and the "B"s were traded back to Lockheed. Now the last RCAF C-119s could be retired. Here 305 shows off on August 31, 1966 at the Canadian International Air Show, Toronto. It wears the glamorous Air Transport Command colour scheme (now replaced by camouflage).

BGen Gordon Diamond (left). As commander of ATG, his was one of the few flying jobs for airforce generals. Here he's with F/O John Barrass, a RAF navigator on exchange with 436 Squadron and nav on Herc 315 which came down to Fredericton on November 28, 1990 with an engine starter for 325 (which had gone u/s the night before).

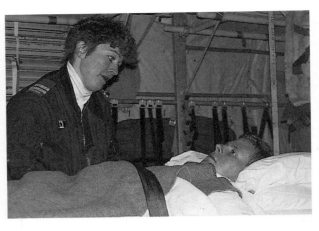

At 0245 on January 15, 1991 Herc 130337 (ATG Flight CF 5355) took off from Doha for Cyprus and Lahr. A few hours later, the Gulf War erupted. Here the crew of 337 poses just before leaving Doha: MCpl Rick Miron (LM 436 Squadron), Capt Pierre Bolduc (AC, 426), MWO Bob Meads (FE, 426), Capt John Stevens (FO, 436) and Maj Hugh MacKay (nav, 436).

Capt Michelle Gagné, a nurse with 313 Field Hospital in Germany, accompanies a medevac patient (injured at sports) aboard the Herc from Qatar to Lahr.

MCpl Miron serves Maj MacKay his hot meal while en route to Cyprus. All the comforts of home aboard ATG.

On the flightdeck of Herc 337 over Saudi Arabia: Capt John Stevens, Capt Pierre Bolduc and the FE, MWO Bob Meads. The roomy Herc cockpit is one of the best ever designed.

At Akrotiri, Cyprus, a 435 crew took over the Herc for the leg to Lahr. The new AC was Capt Frank Berg.

Capt Glenn Northrup of 435 navigates 337 westward down the Med. His father was, at the time, a long-time Herc pilot in ATG.

Herc 337 plods along over the Red Sea, bound for RAF Akrotiri on Cyprus. The sun is rising over the rugged Hejaz region of Saudi Arabia as the big 4000-ehp Allison T-56 turboprops churn away.

Flying down the Med at FL240, Herc 337 passes a C-5 Galaxy heading towards the theatre of war—the fighting was to begin within hours. The C-5 was part of MAC's pipeline of flights throughout the Persian Gulf area. Most of the transports operating during the war were Lockheed C-130s, C-141s and C-5s. Statistics on wartime serviceability show how well each performed: C-130—84%, C-141—86%, C-5—78%.

The view from Flight 5355 over the Alps. The weather was spectacular, but soon the Herc descended into the interminable haze of the Rhine Valley, then made an instrument approach through the murk to land at Lahr—10.9 hours of flying from Qatar.

Above: Kiwi, Canuck and Aussie ground and air crew at "Bulls Eye", one of several multi-national C-130 competitons held around the world. On this occasion the teams competed at CFB Trenton in August 1988.

Below: Herc 317 prepares for a trip from Trenton, April 16, 1991. A 437 Boeing and a Belgian Herc are beyond. The Belgians and Norwegians are often at Trenton —they fly across to use the 426 Squadron C-130 flight simulator.

ATG uses its heavy transports in both tactical and strategic roles. In tactical, crews drop paratroops, deliver heavy loads by LAPES, operate from marginal fields, etc. These skills are practiced at frequent TALEXs—tactical airlift exercises. Here Maj Mike Davis, USAF exchange pilot with 435 Squadron, discusses TALEX matters prior to an April 6, 1991 mission from Trenton. His crewmates are loadmasters MWO Frank MacNeil and WO Harry Grace. The "loadies" manage all drops from the rear of the Herc—a highly demanding task.

Capt Cheryl Almeida, a two-tour Herc pilot with 435, flies 130326 in murky weather during a low level TALEX trip of April 6.

Almeida's crew (sans navigator, Capt Al Baldry) following their mission: WO Brian Wilson (loadie), Capt Rod Misky (pilot), Capt Pete Peterson (base commander's EA), Cheryl, Sgt Earle Dawson and Cpl Ron MacWilliam (loadies) and Sgt Mike Bogdan (FE). Since they work around the open rear of the plane, the loadies wear parachutes. Like nearly all ATG crews, they had worked hard during the recent Gulf War, and were getting back to peace-time duties soon to include such tasks as "Boxtop" (Arctic resupply) and humanitarian aid to Iraq's hapless Kurds.

Maj Mike Davis and Capt Gerry Duhig of 435 Squadron pilot Herc 316 during a TALEX mission from Trenton on April 6, 1991. To the rear is 315 piloted by Maj André Deschamps and Capt Jacques Dufort of 436.

TALEX action on the flight deck as 130326 roars over the countryside north of Trenton at 200 knots / 250' AGL. The 435 crew is all eyes, mapreading and watching for landmarks, keeping on time to the second between turning points. In the right seat is Maj Jim Burger (left seat was Capt John Couch). The nav, Capt Gerry Fraser, is up from his station to check for cues. Exposing for outside then using flash to brighten the cockpit gives even lighting in a picture like this (easier said than done).

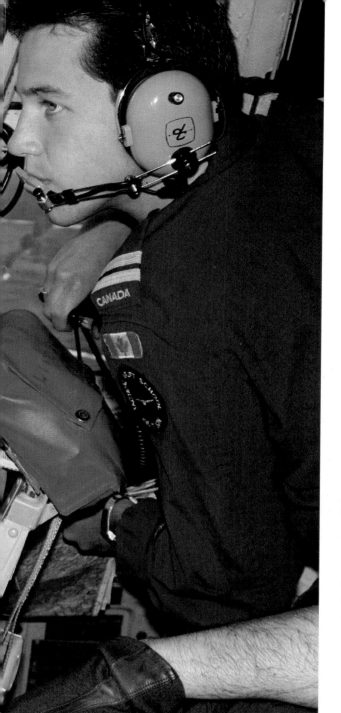

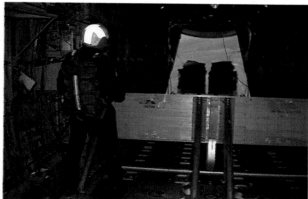

WO Brian Wilson goes over his checklists as he prepares for a heavy drop over Mountain View south of Trenton, then watches his load roll out the Herc's rear door. Here a simple flash allows shooting in the dark interior of the Herc.

In 1990 Ottawa approved the purchase of five C-130H-90s, bringing the ATG fleet to 32. The "H-90s" will be converted for aerial refuelling when funds allow. Here H-90 No. 338 of 435 Squadron sits at Trenton on June 6, 1991.

Before launching the TALEX missions on April 6, many checks are made—including inspections for birds nests high up in the tail. This TALEX ran April 3-10 and involved 15 crews from three squadrons.

Techs at Edmonton service a T-56 engine from one of 435 Squadrons C-130s. Fastidious maintenance keeps the Herc fleet (with some aircraft more than 25 years old) in top shape. On April 7, 1991 of 15 Hercs based in Edmonton, the "oldest" in terms of flying hours was 306 (32,492.6 hrs), the "youngest" was 340 (151.8 hrs). 306 became the first of the SAR Hercs to go to 413 Squadron in mid 1991.

CFB Trenton base badge on the side of a C-130.

DASH 8

AIRCOM has six Boeing/de Havilland Canada Dash 8s. The first two were CC-142s for 412 Det in Lahr where they replaced Dash 7s. In April 1990 they were replaced by a Cosmopolitan and went to 402 Air Reserve Squadron in Winnipeg. They have since been joined by four CT-142 navigation trainers one of which is seen at Hamilton on June 14, 1991. The "CT"s train navigators at the CF Air Navigation School in Winnipeg and are used by the CFS as multi-engine pilot trainers. They have replaced four 429 Squadron C-130Ns. Note the nav radar nose on the CT, which has given rise to the nickname "Gonzo." Complement on the CT is two pilots, two nav instructors and four nav students. Here Gonzo 4 is flown by Capts Marcel Velzil and Brady Aubin with crewman Sgt Bill Ewing, all of 402. Also aboard was Capt Don Pearsons, AIRCOM Heritage Officer.

One of the CC-142s at Lahr in 1988 while with the 412 Squadron detachment on general duties throughout Europe. P&WC PW-120 series engines power the Dash 8.

COSMO

In the late fifties Canadair adapted the Convair 440 from the R-2800 (2500 hp) piston engine to the British Napier Eland 504A (3500 shp) turboprop. The Eland proved a regular nuisance and was replaced in 1966 by the Allison 501-D13 (3750 shp). The original 10 RCAF Convairs were dubbed CC-109 Cosmopolitans, and 7 updated "Cosmos" were still in use in 1991. The first Convair flew in March 1947, so the Cosmo is a real vintage bird. Even so, it delivers valuable service. In this photo, Cosmo 151 of 412 arrives at Trenton on September 22, 1973 carrying Governor General Roland Michener. As the CC-109 has been mainly used by Ottawa civil servants, the nickname "Cosmopolitician" also applies.

Above: Shadows and reflections can be fun subject matter. Here is the well-known Convair/Cosmo plan view (Cosmo 157 at Trenton on August 31, 1972).

Left: Cosmo 152 at Trenton in its 1991 paint scheme.

FALCON

Above: Seven CC-117 Dassault Falcon 20s joined the RCAF in 1967, mostly on civil government VIP duties with 412 Squadron. In the late 1970s three were passed on to 414 in North Bay for electronic warfare training. They took over from 414's EW CF-100s, but were replaced in 1989 by Challengers. In 1990 the fleet was sold to new civil owners. Here the 414 crew of Turnbull, Kay and Sutherland get airborne from Bagotville April 13, 1989.

Centre: Capt Chris Kay and LCol Bill Turnbull during an EW Falcon mission April 11, 1989.

Left: In the back of an EW Falcon, Capt Al Sutherland plays with his knobs and switches, jamming radar and communications of fighters opposing his side during war games from Bagotville in 1990.

Overleaf: These 414 Falcons were at Bagotville in April 1989. The Falcon "bizjet" is one of the all-time beauties in its class. New life has been recently breathed into it with a retrofit kit of new Pratt and Whitney Canada PW305 engines.

CHALLENGER

Above: The Canadair Challenger is AIRCOM's light jet transport. 15 are in service, most with 412 Squadron which has had them since 1983. Several others are with 414, one belongs to AETE at Cold Lake and others are going to MAG on coastal duties. Shown is the first CF Challenger while training at Trenton with 426 Squadron on March 9, 1987.

The crew of Challenger 610 of the 412 Det at Bahrain on January 11, 1991. This one-plane unit began operating the previous October as a 414 Squadron Det flying 606. On December 2, 412 arrived to take over: 3 pilots, 2 flight engineers and 7 techs. The task was "C & L"—communications and liaison. The Challenger flew the Canadian theatre commander and his staff on business throughout the Gulf region and carried priority cargo. There was no hangar space—the techs did all their work on the ramp or under the overhang of the adjacent HAS. The 412 Challenger got home on April 1, 1991, having logged 248 hours in the Gulf.

The Challenger takes on cargo—gas masks for Canadians in Qatar. Nice images on a rainy day.

Spartan conditions—this overhang was where the 412 boys in Bahrain kept their tools, spares and technical manuals. WO Vic Johnson peruses the scene.

A Bahrain International approach plate clipped to the pilot's control column on Challenger 610.

BUFFALO

A 442 Squadron Buffalo at Comox beside a Labrador. The Snowbirds do their thing in the distance. 15 Buffalos joined the air force in 1967, at first with Mobile Command. Soon they moved to SAR and transport squadrons—today they fly with 103 Rescue Unit (Gander), 424 Squadron (Trenton) and 442. The type has been most useful over the years—a solid performer in the SAR world and on Arctic and other projects. By now, the "Buff" is weary—serviceability is a costly and frustrating matter. The air force has decided to retire it ASAP. C-130s will gradually assume its duties.

Buffalo 458 ready to thump down and roar into reverse pitch—a standard STOL landing. The location is Gibson, BC on February 24, 1987.

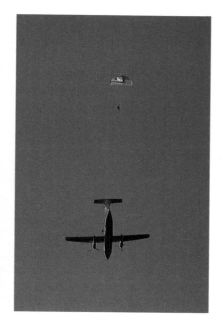

115458 overhead Gibson on pararescue training. Two SARTECHs have just leapt from their perfectly serviceable craft!

Nose art on 458—one baby delivered in flight, two birds written off.

The 442 badge.

The only CF Buffalo lost tragically was 115461. While with 116 ATU at Ismailia, it was shot down on August 9, 1974 by Syrian SAMs while on a UN milk run from Beirut to Damascus. Nine Canadians died in this action—claimed by Syria to have been a mistake. Here 461, then with 424 Squadron, was doing touch-and-goes at Mountain View on June 27, 1973.

The de Havilland Buffalo will fade from ATG service by the mid 1990s. In this April 18, 1991 view with classic British Columbia terrain, 454 nudges in close for photos from 456. By this time, ATG's 10 Buffalos averaged about 15,000 airframe hours. Bill Lamberton's Vampire accompanies 454. Crew on 454 were Capt Mort MacDonnell and Lt Paul Blouin (pilots), Capt Brad White (nav) and MCpl Wayne Webster and Cpl Steve Truesdell (FEs).

TWIN OTTER

The air force purchased nine DHC-6 Twin Otters in 1971. These serve with 440 and 418 Air Reserve Squadrons and No. 4 RSU at CFB Edmonton. The Twin Otter is AIRCOM's only light utility/SAR type and has proven its worth over the years. 801 is on the ramp at Namao on February 18, 1987. On the tail is the 440 Squadron bat emblem and an Eskimo decal. Note the hefty wheel-ski undercarriage.

Twin Otter No. 805, cowlings removed, does an engine run at Namao in April 1991. Its P&WC PT-6 engines are a key reason for the Twin Otter's worldwide success.

Facing page: A mechanic at Namao works on one of Twin Otter 806's PT6 engines.

"THE BOEING"

Since 1970 the Boeing 707 has been ATG's largest transport. Operated by 437 Squadron, it's a real jack-of-all trades, having many configurations for freight, passengers and aerial refuelling. This pair was turning around at Lahr on July 24, 1988. Closest is 704, one of the tankers, but seen *sans* wing tip refuelling pods.

The famous crest of 437 "Husky" Squadron has flown on AIRCOM's five Boeings since 1970. *Omnia Passim* (Anything Anywhere) has proven a most accurate motto for this hard-working squadron.

A 437 Boeing climbs out from Trenton on May 10, 1987. A section of town is below, the base is beyond, then the waters of the Bay of Quinte. The Boeing's mighty Pratt & Whitney JT3D turbofans are set to climb, throttled back from their 100% 18,000 pound take-off setting of a few minutes earlier.

Much of 437's work entails "trash hauling"—carrying thousands of tons of freight on the world's airways. A load may be in support of an Army exercise, supplies and equipment for Canada's NATO operation, cargo destined for a UN deployment, or humanitarian aid for the victims of some flood or earthquake in a remote corner of the world. This scene shows part of the in- and outbound airfreight at CFB Lahr on July 24, 1988.

A hefty load of palletized freight trundles on a K-25 loader from the 5AMU warehouse at Lahr, then is seen about to be gobbled up by a 707 for the trip to Trenton. ATG's 707s are -320Cs, the passenger-freight "combi" edition with a 7' x 11' cargo door and all-freight capacity of 45 tons. The grandaddy of the 707 was the Model 367-80 which first flew on July 15, 1954. Its derivatives have been in steady production ever since.

Air-to-air refuelling (AR) is a vital 437 task. Aircraft 703 and 704 were modified for this role in 1971. Here 703 departs Trenton on June 23, 1990. Note its wingtip AR pods, developed in conjunction with Beech Aircraft, Boeing and the CF. The tankers work hard month by month to keep fighter pilots current in AR. In 1991 the two tankers were serving 410, 416, 419 and 441 Squadrons at Cold Lake, 425 and 433 at Bagotville and 421 and 439 at Baden. The Boeings' workload was eased in 1990 when AIRCOM curtailed its trans-Canada "airline" schedule—for many years they had provided weekly service from Shearwater to Comox. The Comox-Vancouver and Trenton-Ottawa legs were hardly suited to the mighty Boeings, and helped pile up undue landings and takeoffs, shortening their useful lives. In the Gulf War the Boeing fleet logged 3000 hours, including 558 on AR ops (500,000-plus gallons pumped to fighters).

Chartering and leasing are trends in the DND. This began in the 1980s with chartered Worldways DC-8s. Here SF712, a Nationair DC-8, turns around at Winnipeg on April 10, 1990.

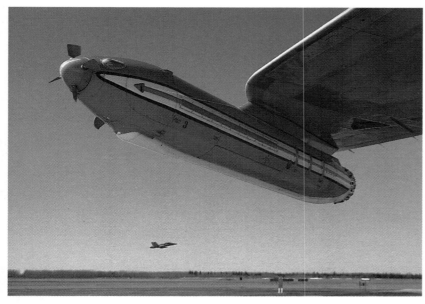

The Beech Model 1080 AR pod in stowed configuration. On the nose is a ram air generator that boosts fuel flow from 150 to 300 gallons per minute. It actuates once the receiving fighter has contact and has pushed back a specified length of hose. The pod is 17' long, 25" in diameter and attaches to the wing's extended main spar at three points. It houses 35' of hose with a metal basket at its extremity to guide in the receiver's AR probe. The pod weighs 800 pounds.

Aboard 703 during AR training (April 3, 1989), Majs Crawford and Prystai and WO Chaisson (FE) chat during a relaxing few moments.

Capt Dave Alexander instructs two trainee AR navs, Lts Simon Round and Steve Smith.

Old time AR nav, Maj Don Bengert, and Capt Denis Blanchet man the port AR station in the rear of 703. They are observing CF-18s off the wing. The observers will bring the jets on and off the hose using voice, or coded lights in the baskets.

Now the flight deck is really busy. Ken Hill has taken over the FE panel and he and Bob Forgues are exchanging ideas. On the left, navigators Denis Blanchet and Steve Smith (seated) are at work. Why such a crowd? On many a flight, extras are on board training as new crew or on refreshers.

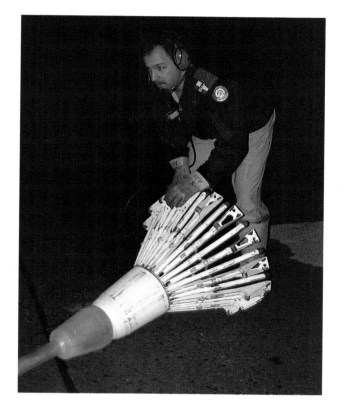

MCpl Joe Walsh, a pod maintenance tech, inspects the port AR basket on 703 following a mission at Cold Lake on April 4, 1989.

THE DAK

The Douglas DC-3/C-47/Dakota was the longest-serving RCAF/AIRCOM type (1943–89). Here "Pinocchio" (12959, ex RCAF 979), one of AIRCOM's last Dakotas, departs Trenton in July 1986. Delivered to the RCAF on November 18, 1944, it served on such units as 414 Squadron and 109 Composite Unit. In 1964 it became a trainer with a CF-104 navigation system. It was with Base Flight in Cold Lake 1976–86, then finished its career with CFS/402 Squadron in Winnipeg.

Through the early postwar era many RCAF aircraft wore distinctive schemes and unit markings. Dakota KN448 was seen at Malton on April 20, 1960 with a flashy red airline stripe, and the "LK" code and tail logo of Air Materiel Command from Ottawa. KN448 was originally delivered to the RCAF (436 Sqn) in October 1945. In all, the RCAF/CF had some 169 Dakotas—they served in many roles for nearly 46 years!

"Dak" 988 lands at Toronto Island Airport on August 31, 1966. It had joined the RCAF in April 1945 and later carried tail number 12961. Still later, it served as CF-TTZ and was last known in the markings of Ontario Central Airlines. Its registration was cancelled in 1974.

"Z2-B" are the 437 Squadron markings on 12944 (ex FZ671), another AIR-COM Dakota. It had been delivered to the RAF on February 4, 1944 where it served with 48 Squadron. It joined 437 in September 1945 and was with such units as 426, 429, 435, 437, 25 Ambulance and No. 1 ANS through the years. Upon retirement it got its final posting—to the base museum at CFB Comox where it is seen in this photo.

ATC – THE GOOD OLD DAYS

Air Transport Command's heavy transport through the 1950s was the Canadair North Star, a modified Douglas C-54 built in Montreal for the RCAF, TCA and BOAC. The North Star was the backbone of the RCAF's Korean War airlift, making 599 trips between McChord AFB (in Washington) and Japan. The North Star was retired in December 1965. For several years, old North Stars served as tramp freighters. 17514 became CF-SVP-X of the National Aeronautical Establishment. For years it flew on geophysical projects around the world gathering, among other material, vast amounts of data about sea floor spreading/plate tectonics. The NAE retired SVP in 1978 and a Miami group acquired it. It was the last flying North Star, working in the illegal drug smuggling trade. When last seen it was derelict on Greater Inagua Island. Here it is with the NAE at Trenton on June 22, 1973 for the 25th anniversary of ATC. Note its magnetic anomaly detector (MAD) boom.

The RCAF's "Queen of the Skies" was the one and only Canadair C-5, built as a VIP transport for 412 Squadron. It was on strength 1950-1966. The C-5 carried royalty and other heads of state on domestic and global tours. It was eventually sold in California and scrapped in Long Beach. Here it was in storage at Mountain View in June 1966. Note its P & W R-2800 radials vs the North Star's in-line R-R Merlins.

The RCAF began operating de Havilland Comets in 1953, the first air force with jet transports. They performed general duties with 412 Squadron, but frequently were also high speed targets for NORAD's CF-100s. The Comets were retired to Mountain View in 1965, and ultimately scrapped. This photo shows CF-SVR, two ex-RCAF Comets in one! They were purchased from CADC by a dealer who combined them to make one good airframe. He supposedly had a buyer in Peru but the sale was embargoed by Ottawa. SVR was scrapped in Florida. Here it is seen at Mount Hope, May 13, 1967.

To replace its aging North Stars, the RCAF purchased Canadair CC-106 Yukons, 10 for 437 Squadron, two for 412. These did yeoman service from 1959 to 1971 when they were replaced by the 707. Here Yukon 929 of 437 Squadron, its mighty Rolls-Royce Tynes throttled back, crosses the threshold at Trenton *circa* 1961.

Yukons 922, 925 and 929 with their lone Sabre escort fly over Toronto during the CIAS *circa* 1962.

The Fairchild C-119 Flying Box Car hauled freight and troops with the RCAF 1952 - 1967. It was a typical "anything anywhere" transport with ATC. First flown in 1947, a total of 1112 were built by 1955 for various governments. The RCAF operated 35 and suffered but one fatality—a paratrooper killed at Borden when his chute hung up. The C-119 was powered by reliable Wright R-3350s of 3400 hp. All-up weight was 74,400 lb, max speed 296 mph and max range 3480 miles (vs 135,000 lb, 385 mph and 4000 miles for the C-130B). When sold by CADC in the 1970's, many ex-RCAF C-119s became forest fire bombers in the US. Some operated into the late 1980s.

A North Star leads a Cosmo and a C-119 over Toronto for the CIAS, *circa* 1961.

A great postwar workhorse was the Avro Lancaster MK10. The "Lanc," first flown January 9, 1941, became one of Bomber Command's stalwarts. 430 were licence-built by Victory Aircraft at Malton, with the first flying August 1, 1943. Many of these served overseas. Postwar they were ASW patrol bombers, navigation trainers, photo-mapping platforms and SAR aircraft. FM219 was with 111 Composite Unit at Winnipeg when photographed on September 4, 1961. It was scrapped at Dunnville, Ontario, in the spring of 1965. In the photo below, AR Lanc KB839 of 408 Squadron (Rockcliffe) gets up and away from Trenton on July 1, 1961. 408's Lancs did most of the high Arctic photo-mapping in the 1950's. KB839 is on display at CFB Greenwood.

FM104 and KB976 at Downsview for the RCAF Lancaster phase-out ceremony on April 5, 1964. FM104 was in from Torbay where it had served with 107 Rescue Unit. Today it perches on a pylon on Toronto's waterfront, gradually rotting out. It had been overseas briefly in 1945 with 408 and 428 Squadrons. KB976 had initially been assigned in 1945 to 405 Squadron. Here it is with 408 (Photo) Squadron (it had a 3-foot nose extension, the MK10 Arctic Reconnaissance version). Later, KB976 was a water bomber in Alberta and the NWT, then joined the Strathallan Collection in Scotland as G-BCOH. At press time it was being refurbished following damage from a hangar collapse.

KB943 and FM224 being scrapped at Dunnville in March 1965.

DHC-3 "Steam Otters" of No. 2 Air Reserve Wing, Toronto, visit CFB North Bay for the Canada Day airshow in 1977. Sixty-nine Otters served the RCAF/CF from 1953 to 1982. Useful for a hundred and one tasks, the Otter was at home on land, water or snow (also in the air!). De Havilland built 466 Otters and at least half are still at work. The Canadian Northland, US Northwest and Alaska are home for most. Numerous PT-6 turboprop and Polish PZL engine conversions have been done in recent years, giving added life to the vintage DHC design.

VR-3661 at Trenton on wheel-skis, December 27, 1960. This was the 7th Otter built and the first for the RCAF (delivered March 28, 1953). It worked with CEPE at Rockcliffe and Churchill, went to 408 Squadron, then to 102 Communications Unit at Trenton in July 1960. In April 1963 it was donated to the Indian Air Force as BM-1004 and was still active 20 years later. Note the Canadian Ensign on the fin. About this time it was replacing the old tricolour finflash as the standard national marking on the RCAF fleet.

The RCAF's post war answer to the Avro Anson was the Beechcraft Model 18 Expeditor (alias "Exploder", "Bug Smasher", etc). This versatile light twin was a pilot and nav trainer, a VIP plane and all 'round utility workhorse—on search and rescue, getting around to weekend parties, etc. 5198 (TOS February 11, 1953) was one of the last airforce Beech 18s (394 in all) and was at Camp Borden on June 21, 1968. A few months later the last were turned over to CADC for disposal. Many served in the bush for years thereafter with civil operators and a few are still kicking around.

Navy "Bug Smasher" 2312 flies into Dorval on a "comm" flight, May 22, 1961.

The STOL DHC-4 Caribou was first flown at Toronto in 1958. Most of the 307 built went to the US Army and many served in Viet Nam. The others were mainly exported, but the RCAF took nine. These were used on such UN operations as Kashmir, Yemen and the Sinai. In 1971 Canada gave its Caribous to Tanzania. Here 5323, Caribou No. 12, sits at Trenton on June 11, 1966. A few ex-RCAF Caribous have since trickled back across the Atlantic, some to work in the clandestine Central American market.

The RCAF was renowned for its search and rescue expertise. This developed from the 1920s and was greatly perfected during WW II. Postwar, the RCAF operated several SAR units with the Dakota, Canso, Lancaster, Norseman, Otter and early helicopters such as the H-5. In 1960 a new type was added—the Grumman SA-16 (RCAF destination: CSR-110) Albatross. Ten operated from Greenwood, Trenton and Comox. The "Albert" was a typical Grumman design—solid as a rock. When the Alberts were retired in 1970, the CF was out of the flying boat business for the first time since 1924. Here 9304 runs up at Trenton on June 11, 1966.

The Canso was the RCAF's SAR Trojan in the postwar years. It plugged along until finally replaced by the Albatross in April 1962. Here 9830 (QZ, from Trenton) flies near Toronto on September 10, 1960. When sold by CADC it became a water bomber (CF-PQK) with the Quebec government. Several ex-RCAF Cansos are still earning their keep.

Many RCAF aircrew served on the North American B-25 Mitchell bomber during the war. In peacetime the RCAF had more than 150 Mitchells, mainly for training airborne intercept (AI) navigators but also on general duties. KL148, landing at Downsview on July 7, 1960, was a personnel transport with Air Materiel Command. It was originally USAAF 43-3634, delivered on September 17, 1943. It flew in combat in Italy and was turned over to the RCAF October 18, 1944, serving at No. 5 OTU. Postwar it served as a nav trainer at Winnipeg, with 418 Squadron and with AMC. It was SOS May 18, 1962, was stored at Dunnville, sold and became CF-NWV. It languished at St. Thomas, Ontario until sold into the US in 1969. In 1991 it was operating from Detroit as NX3774—a fully restored warbird.

AURORA

Aurora 140117 taxis at Comox as a Buff and Lab of 442 Squadron make a sprightly departure, April 5, 1990. Canada's version of the Lockheed P-3 Orion, the Aurora is one of the world's advanced ASW aircraft. Fourteen serve at Greenwood with 404, 405 and 415 Squadrons (plus the Maritime Proving and Evaluation Unit) while four are at Comox with 407. Besides their primary role, the Auroras work for other government departments on such tasks as fisheries enforcement, anti-drug smuggling surveillance, wildlife surveys, and search and rescue. Each logs about 1000 hours yearly. The high time Aurora on December 17, 1990 was 140109 with 10,131 hours.

Front end crew on Aurora 109 for an eight-hour "fishpat" (Type 9 fisheries patrol) on December 17, 1990. Capt Brian Keene (top photo) was the AC. FO was Lt John Baird (centre photo). Joining the crew for a re-currency trip (following a ground tour) was Maj Rick Anscombe (bottom photo). Brian and John were first-tour pipeliners, and typical of many new CF pilots. They each arrived at Portage for primary flying holding commercial flying licences (in "the old days" most aspiring airforce pilots were green—right off the street, never having flown before). Rick was the old hand on the crew—an ex-Royal Canadian Navy Tracker pilot (Hercs and Auroras later). For such cockpit photos, a wideangle zoom lens is a great help. 24–35mm usually suffices.

The indispensable FE on 109's fishpat was Sgt Rocky Hendrickson. His day's work began at 0500 with the crew at the mission briefing. Then came the detailed Aurora technical preflight—the FE's job is to guarantee that the aircraft is ready to fly. On this day, all went well for the FE until strap-in time when he found that his own seat was u/s! Once that was rectified (included was a careful FOD check for a missing nut and bolt), 109 was airborne at 0900. For the rest of the day Rocky was busy monitoring aircraft systems, keeping detailed charts and setting power time after time as the pilots made "ident" passes over foreign fishing vessels along Canada's 200-mile economic zone boundary south and east of Newfoundland.

At 1025 hours Capt Keene "loitered" No. 1. This is a fuel-saving practice on overwater patrols. The Aurora cruised "on three" for the next several hours as it inspected fishing boats. Most targets were large European and Soviet trawlers. The first was acquired at 1040 hours by the Aurora's FLIR 30 miles away at 43° 31'N, 51° 57'W. Quickly, three more ships were picked up at 58nm and found to be fishing legally 8 to 10 miles outside Canada's limit. So it went for the rest of the day as 109 worked steadily in perfect weather, cruising at 200', popping up to 1000' or so only to pick up new targets.

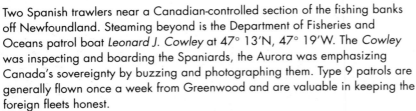

Two Spanish trawlers near a Canadian-controlled section of the fishing banks off Newfoundland. Steaming beyond is the Department of Fisheries and Oceans patrol boat *Leonard J. Cowley* at 47° 13'N, 47° 19'W. The *Cowley* was inspecting and boarding the Spaniards, the Aurora was emphasizing Canada's sovereignty by buzzing and photographing them. Type 9 patrols are generally flown once a week from Greenwood and are valuable in keeping the foreign fleets honest.

On an "ident" pass on Type 9 patrols, the Aurora overflies a vessel from the stern. On the flight deck all crew watch for the vessel's name, home port and ID registration letters. Just behind the cockpit, observers on the left and right do the same. In the rear, two more are spotting. In this way, a vessel's ID is confirmed and whether or not it is fishing, underway, etc. Here one of the starboard spotters, Lt Lee, prepares to ID a ship, then radio his observations to the flightdeck.

REUNION 91

A wonderful historic occasion for AIRCOM was Reunion 91 (May 30–June 2) at CFB Greenwood. It brought together 404, 405 and 415 Squadrons and VP International (the worldwide association of ASW partners). More than 2500 attended. One of many events was a Wing Parade. Here the Base Commander, Col K.R. Allen, leads part of the parade past the reviewing stand where the Deputy Commander AIR-COM, MGen P.J. O'Donnell, took the salute.

Some of the ASW aircraft representing VPI at its 25th anniversary celebration during Reunion 91. Aircraft of eight nations attended. Seen here are the Portuguese P-3B, AIRCOM Aurora, German Atlantique, Spanish P-3B, Dutch P-3C and two US Navy P-3Cs.

Squadron Colours are displayed during the Reunion 91 parade. The AIRCOM Band plays in the background.

415 Squadron parades its Colours.

Members of the AIRCOM Band march past.

Aurora 112 flown by an MP&EU crew completes a fly-past for the Reunion crowd.

Several generations of ASW and anti-shipping crews mingled over the week-end. In this jolly group is (left) 1Lt Derrick Hotte, a young navigator with 415 Squadron. Next are Dr. Al Hildebrand (pilot), Lew Rowe (nav) and Keith Mailman (WOp/AG), all of whom were on Hampden bomber ops in the early days of 415 Squadron in WWII. Right is aviation artist Geoff Bennett, who flew the Argus on 404 and 415 Squadrons. Gatherings such as Reunion 91 go a long way in strengthening the great traditions of Canada's air force.

Greenwood boasts a fine historic ASW trio—a Lockheed P2V-7 Neptune, a Canadair Argus and an Avro Lancaster.

The squadrons were right into the spirit of things at Reunion 91. These 415 Aurora aircrew were in authentic WWII RCAF uniforms. In real life they are MCpl Denis Aucoin, Maj Rodney Ward and Sgt Brian Gracie. "Falstaff" is the mascot.

A/V/M R.J. "Reg" Lane, one of the RCAF's leading wartime fliers, attended Reunion 91. He commanded 405 (Pathfinder) Squadron, June–August 1944, and earned the DSO and DFC with Bar. Postwar he headed Air Transport Command and No.1 Air Division Europe.

SEA KING

The CH-124 Sea King has been Canada's shipboard ASW helicopter since 1963. Forty-one were built, mainly by Pratt & Whitney Canada. Besides its primary role, the Sea King has been valuable in search and rescue, and in communications and transport work. It serves mainly from Shearwater with 406 (Helicopter Training) and 423 Squadrons, and the Helicopter Operational Test and Evaluation Flight, and from Victoria with 443 Squadron. In 1990-91 Sea Kings were in the Persian Gulf for several months. These from 406 were at Shearwater on December 17, 1990. In the photo at left, Sea King 423 was shot from an Argus. The chopper was over Lake Ontario during the CIAS on August 31, 1972.

Above: The Sea King fleet is maintained at Shearwater by BAMEO and at Halifax International Airport by IMP Aerospace. This view shows aircraft during periodic maintenance in the BAMEO hangar. Almost overnight BAMEO organized and implemented a big Sea King mod program for the Persian Gulf operation.

Facing page: Sea King and Aurora DLIR underway at IMP. Aircraft are stripped down to the bare bones in a program taking several months. They leave the shops as close to "like new" as any 25-year-old helicopter can be.

In July 1989 MAG moved HS443 to the West Coast, making it the first MAG Sea King operation in the Pacific region. In February 1991, 443 opened its new facility at Victoria International Airport. The squadron has about 120 personnel and six Sea Kings. It provides two detachments to serve on HMCSs *Huron, Annapolis* and *Provider*. In this view, Sea King 406 winds up at Victoria for a training mission. Although long in the teeth, Canada's Sea Kings will serve well into the 1990s as a replacement is sought.

Sea King 4013 in its RCN scheme of June 1965. It was seen at RCAF Station Rockcliffe.

THE GRUMMAN IRONWORKS

A pair of RCN ASW Grumman Trackers (1545, 1577) visiting Trenton on August 28, 1969. In 1991 both these aircraft were still on strength at the CF School of Aerospace Engineering and Technology.

Left: Three 880 (MR) Squadron CP-121 Trackers get ready for some flying at Shearwater on August 12, 1975. By this time, the Tracker had given up ASW and was moving into its new career in fisheries patrol (Canada had declared its 200-mile economic zone in 1975, giving renewed life to the Tracker).

Facing page: Seen from an Argus, Trackers 183 and 155 bank sharply over Prince Edward County near Trenton on August 31, 1972. The Tracker became a solid fixture in Canada, first joining the Royal Canadian Navy in 1956, and not retiring until 1990. It was the RCN's primary ASW aircraft, serving aboard HMCS Bonaventure until 1969.

The old Grumman Avenger was replaced in the RCN by the Grumman Tracker. This Tracker was caught landing at Downsview *circa* 1960. Aircraft 1562 (facing page) carries 5" HVARs and was at Oshawa for a breakfast fly-in on June 15, 1962. No. 1562 was first taken on strength November 13, 1965 (by VS880). It went to VU32 in 1967, AMDU in June 1969, and CFSATE January 14, 1970, by when it had flown about 4600 hours. It was still at Borden in 1991. These rugged aircraft are sometimes said to be products of the "Grumman Ironworks."

Below: Tracker 173 of 880 Squadron coughs and wheezes as its Wright R-1820s turn over on a frigid early morning at Summerside, January 14, 1987. When the Trackers left service in 1990, AIR-COM retired its last large piston engines.

Carrying a SKAD (Survival Kit Air Droppable) on the starboard wing , 173
lands at Downsview (CFB Toronto) on August 20, 1987.

The 30th anniversary Tracker visiting Downsview with 173 on August 20. It
toured the country through 1987, bringing back memories of a great era.

Tracker 181 of VU-33 ready to fly a fisheries patrol at Comox, August 18, 1983.

C-GTRT (ex-12185) was the prototype turboprop Tracker created by IMP Aerospace of Halifax. Loaned from 880 Squadron, TRT first flew on September 15, 1988 with Pratt & Whitney Canada PT6A-67AFs of 1424 shp replacing the standard 1525 hp Wright R-1820 radials. There was interest in converting the fleet to PT6s, but Ottawa's 1989 budget suddenly eliminated the Tracker, along with its base at Summerside. IMP has since introduced a PT6 program for Brazil's Tracker fleet, and Conair in BC has converted several fire fighting Trackers to PT6s.

In 1990 Atlantic Aviation of St. John's took over the Tracker fisheries task. It flies King Air 200s with advanced electronics and radar. Its three King Airs flew 1000-plus hours in the first year. This one was at Halifax on June 2, 1991, just in from a patrol.

While MAG today operates its sophisticated ASW Auroras and Sea Kings, and dreams of the EH-101, this was Canada's big ASW aircraft 35-40 years ago—the wartime Grumman Avenger. This pair was returning to Downsview from an exercise on March 12, 1960. They belonged to VC-920, one of the RCN reserve squadrons of the era. This version was designated the AS-3M by the RCN. Most ex-RCN Avengers went on to careers as sprayers and water bombers. A few are still airworthy.

Avenger 908 (USN serial number 53697) of VC-920 was caught at Downsview November 7, 1959. It has underwing sonar and MAD gear in the tail boom. Note the weapons hardpoints under wing and the arrester gear. 908 was TOS July 25, 1952, and SOS July 5, 1960. It later became CF-LEH and operated in New Brunswick for many years as a spray plane.

CF-MSX, ex-RCN 53496. It was sold as surplus in 1960 and began firefighting and spraying for Skyways. It came into Cartierville on May 22, 1961 in a gaggle of 10 Avengers headed for bud-worm spraying in New Brunswick. On July 7, 1961, it crashed while working near Harrison Lake, B.C.

NEPTUNE

Superseding the ASW Lancaster and filling the gap till the Argus entered service was the Lockheed P2V-7 Neptune. Produced 1944 - 1961, the Neptune was a solid performer with its R-3350s and retrofitted J-34 jet engines. The RCAF operated 25, the last leaving from 407 Squadron in Comox in 1968. This one, in its ominous midnight blue scheme, was shot at Trenton May 28, 1960. It was in from No. 2 (Maritime) Operational Training Unit at Summerside. Today a few ex-RCAF Neptunes are fire bombers in the US.

ARGUS

The Argus fleet served 1957-1982. There were 33 of these ASW monsters and all but two survived a 25-year career. Many were scrapped with advent of the Aurora in 1980. Some were saved for posterity and may be seen at Summerside, Greenwood, Ottawa (NAM) and Comox. Winnipeg's Western Canada Aviation Museum has one in storage, and another is at Mountain View where it has been a useful prop in training anti-terrorist specialists. Here 10718 of 407 Squadron prepares at Cold Lake for an eight-hour NORPAT over the central Arctic islands on March 22, 1977.

Argus 718 casts its shadow over bleak Arctic terrain at 68° 10'N, 106° 36'W. This was a March 24, 1977 inspection visit to the Hope Bay Mine (seen here) to check on activity there. Hope Bay appeared abandoned for the winter.

Heritage has always been one of AIR-COM's priorities. On April 10, 1991 it hosted a gathering to honour F/L David Hornell who earned the Victoria Cross during Coastal Command operations on June 24, 1944. Hornell and crew (162 Squadron, RCAF) that day attacked and sank *U-1225* in the North Atlantic. Their Canso was itself shot down. Three of the eight man crew, Hornell included, eventually died of exposure during 21 hours in the water before help arrived. In this group photo on April 10 are Ash and Bill Hornell (David's cousin and brother), Ed Matheson (Hornell's navigator), LGen Fred Sutherland (Commander AIRCOM), Graham Campbell (radio operator), Mrs. Stephanie Holowaty (sister of P/O Andrew Mynarski, VC), Sydney Cole (wireless operator) and Mary Hornell (Bill's wife). Behind is a portrait of Hornell and a painting by Graham Wragg of his fatal action. On this occasion, the Hornell family presented David's VC to AIRCOM for display.

Below: Canada's only naval jet fighter was the McDonnell F2H-3 Banshee which served aboard HMCS *Bonaventure* and from Shearwater from 1955 to 1962. This one is preserved at Shearwater.

VERTOLS

The RCAF was early to recognize the usefulness of helicopters. It began flying them with the Sikorsky H-5 (S-51) in 1947, and soon added the Sikorsky H-19 (S-55), and H-34 (S-58), and Vertol 44. 9639 was one of 20 RCAF "44"s used 1954 - 1968. It did great utility work on the Mid Canada Line and in SAR, even though most such early helicopters had limited power/payload. The 44 was the final version of the Piasecki H-21 and could carry a useful load of $1^1/2$ - 2 tons. 9639 was seen at Trenton on June 8, 1968 with the first RCAF Vertol 107 Labrador in the background. The 44 was on its way out, the 107 was its replacement. Note the general family resemblance with the 44, 107 and the bigger CH-47 Chinook. This heritage dates back to Frank Piasecki's twin rotor concept of the early 1940s.

Most RCAF Vertol 44s were operated for the DND by civilian companies once construction on the Mid Canada Line was finished in 1957. The survivors mostly ended up in junkyards. These were shot at Mountain View on June 26, 1971 in their basic RCAF colours with civil registrations and Dominion Helicopters titles.

The Labrador entered Canadian service in 1963. Eighteen were ordered for Mobile Command and the RCAF. The "MobCom" ones were then known as Voyageurs. All 14 surviving examples have been standardized for SAR and serve with 103RU and 413, 424 and 442 Squadrons. Over the decades they have rescued many from peril, including from foundering ships. Here Lab 302 of 442 Squadron sits at Comox on March 18, 1977 as a 408 Twin Huey departs.

Overleaf: Voyageur 410 in its Army scheme lifts off from a temporary helipad at the Canadian National Exhibition in Toronto, September 3, 1971.

Facing page, top: The Labrador on the previous pages in maintenance at Comox nearly 20 years later.

424 Labrador No. 308 off Trenton on June 11, 1991. It was conducting SAR training with CCG *Spindrift*, a 68-foot cutter from Cobourg on Lake Ontario.

The three 447 Chinooks seen for the last time at CFB Edmonton, April 8, 1991. The Army's "heavy hooker" helicopter, the Chinook served 1974–1991. Two crashed over the years, and the remaining seven were well worn. Discussions about modernizing the fleet to CH-47D specs had gone on for years, but Ottawa chose instead to phase out the Chinooks in 1991—447 Squadron closed on April 30, 450 converted to Hueys later that summer.

"Hooker 4" required a last minute engine change prior to departure for Mountain View on April 10. Its odd-ball Lycoming T55-L-11C was one reason for the Chinook's demise in 10 TAG, as was its metal rotor blades (vs the more serviceable glassfibre ones). In this view the 400-pound rescue hoist can be seen over the front entrance. It too was unique to the CH-147.

Welcome to 447—the Squadron doesn't live here anymore.

An impromptu "class photo" at 447 Squadron on April 8. Two days later 447 launched its last mission— Hooker 4 to Ottawa.

CH-147007 (Hooker 7) departing Edmonton on April 8, 1991. Crewed by Maj Pete Krayer, Capt Clark Jule, MCpl Jay Orcutt and Cpl Brian Medland (FEs) and MCpl Mario Langlois (LM), 007 was the first of 447 Squadron's Chinooks to leave for Mountain View once the demise of the Chinook fleet was announced on February 19.

The pilots on Hooker 5 (LCol Dave Lowdon and Capt Ross Wuerth) get their met briefing from Sgt Sam McMullen before departing Edmonton on April 9. LCol Lowdon was 447's last CO. He wears the original 447 (SAM) Squadron patch —447 (SAM) had been his first posting as an officer cadet. He later flew TACHEL with 408 and 427 and Buffalos with 424, then flew in the Sinaii (MFO). In 1990 he was CO of the 89th RWAU before rejoining 447 in 1987. Capt Wuerth joined the forces in 1978 and flew with 403 before being posted to 447 in 1988. Both he and the CO also had postings to Fort Rucker, the US Army's big helicopter base in Alabama. There Wuerth became a CH-47D IP and qualified on NVGs— all typical of the great training and experience of AIRCOM's personnel.

The crew on Hooker 5 April 9-12: Capt Ross Wuerth, LCol Dave Lowdon, MCpl Bill Johnson (FE), Sgt Phil Levesque (LM) and Larry Milberry ("crew biographer"). Flying time on their Edmonton— Ottawa ferry was 16 hours.

An ideal way to see Canada close-up is from a low flying helicopter. Here are two typical scenes from Hooker 5—Tramping Lake, Saskatchewan on April 9, and the north shore of Lake Superior near Wawa two days later.

Hooker 5 approaches to land at Thunder Bay, April 10. The 447 fleet had the following airframe hours prior to ferrying east: Hooker 4—6936, Hooker 5—7041, Hooker 7—7555.8. Canada's were apparently the world's high-time Chinooks.

The 450 Squadron Chinook "doing its thing". In this case, it's 003 doing a demo at the 1978 CIAS. Some feel that Canada has lost a valuable national resource with phase-out of the Chinooks—they have proven their worth as heavy lifters during floods and forest fires, were valuable during the 1990 crisis at Oka, and were longterm SAR resources in the "Majaid" (major air disaster) role at Edmonton. For now, Canada is without these services, although the coffers will be better off without the extravagant Chinook operating expenses.

KIOWA & JET RANGER

Canada's standard observation, light utility, and training helicopter is the Bell CH-136 Kiowa. A fleet of 74 was purchased in 1971 to replace the Hiller UH-12 and Cessna L-19 in Army observation units. Most are still in use, although many have been rebuilt over the years following prangs. The original Basic Helicopter School Kiowas were passed on to the Air Reserves when the BHS received new Jet Rangers in 1981. Here a 400 Squadron Kiowa flies along the Lake Ontario shore in east end Toronto on November 26, 1988 with Maj Kevin Psutka and Lt Mike McKay aboard.

"Triple Four" Bell Kiowas on the line at their home base in Lahr, West Germany July 8, 1982. Long a CFE resource, 444 now comes under 10TAG.

The folks in 10TAG get to know Canada close up. This was the view straight ahead from Kiowa 203 as it worked its way up the spectacular Val Cartier river valley on the way from St. Hubert to Bagotville on February 12, 1987. LCol Jean Guimond was flying.

In 1989 the BHS loaned some of its Jet Rangers to the 89th RWAU for UN duties in Honduras/Nicaragua. They provided C & L while the Contra rebels were being demobilized. Here Jet Ranger 314 is at Tegucigalpa along with Alouette IIIs of Evergreen Helicopters. The 89th returned to Canada in December 1990, its job completed in Central America.

HUEYS

In 1968 MobCom got 10 Bell CH-118 (UH-IH) Hueys. These were originally operated by 403 Squadron at Petawawa. Mainly for Army use in the air-mobile role, the Hueys were a great success and soon 50 improved CH-135 Twin Hueys were ordered, powered by the Pratt & Whitney Canada PT6 TwinPac. Nine CH-118s were still in service in 1991 and for years have been in the "base flight" role—utility and SAR. Today they are spread among Bagotville, Cold Lake and Moose Jaw (home of the Huey OTU). Here Huey 102 thumps along the flightline at Bagotville, April 12, 1989.

"Single Huey" 106 visiting North Bay from Bagotville on July 1, 1977 in its short-lived red and white SAR paint job.

Overleaf: Base Flight Hueys 103 and 110 at Cold Lake on April 4, 1989. No. 110 is having an engine change—both Lycoming T-53 turbine engines (one coming, one going) are on their stands. The base flight Hueys serve many useful roles, including medevac. In the late 1980s the fleet underwent a tail rotor mod to improve control authority.

135147, a standard CH-135 Twin Huey, at Summerside on January 14, 1987. This was one of VU-32s machines, since reassigned to SERT Flight in Ottawa for combined forces tactical duties with the RCMP.

An AETE CH-135 (135126) at Cold Lake on March 25, 1977.

One of the three SAR Twin Hueys used by 424 Squadron and later with Base Flight at Goose Bay. In 1990 they were tested with external long-range fuel tanks. 135114 was photographed at Trenton on September 10, 1983.

408 Squadron is 10 TAG's only operation in Western Canada—it flies from Edmonton with Kiowas and Twin Hueys. Here Maj Tony MacDougall and crew set off on a Twin Huey mission on the morning of April 9, 1991 as two Kiowas form a backdrop.

Twin Huey 145 gets a good going over from a crew of 408 techs.

From 1948-1973 Canada's "army aviators" flew fixed wing air observation with Austers and Cessna L-19s. Some of the rugged L-19s remain in service as glider tow planes for the Air Cadet training program. This example was working from Comox in 1991 with the B.C. regional cadet operation.

APPENDICES

CANADIAN AIR FORCE ORGANIZATION 1991

Headquarters	Winnipeg
Fighter Group	North Bay
Maritime Air Group	Halifax
10 Tactical Air Group	St. Hubert
Air Transport Group	Trenton
Training	Winnipeg
1 Canadian Air Division	Lahr
AETE	Cold Lake

AIRCOM AIRCRAFT IN MID-1991

Designation Codes: CC – transport, CE – electronic warfare, CF – fighter, CH – helicopter, CP – maritime patrol fixed wing, CT – trainer, ET – electronic warfare.

Type	Name	Quantity	Squadrons	Base(s)
CC-109	Cosmopolitan	7	412	Ottawa
			412 (Det)	Colorado Springs
				Lahr
CH-113	Labrador	14	103RU	Gander
			413	Greenwood
			424	Trenton
			442	Comox
CT-114	Tutor	146	2CFFTS	Moose Jaw
			Snowbirds	Moose Jaw
			CFSATE	Borden
			CFS	Winnipeg
			FIS	Portage la Prairie
			AETE	Cold Lake
CC-115	Buffalo	10	424	Trenton
			442	Comox
CF-116	Freedom Fighter	84	419	Cold Lake
			AETE	Cold Lake
			CFSATE	Borden
CH-118	Iroquois	9	Base Flight	Bagotville
				Moose Jaw
				Cold Lake
CP-121	Tracker	5	CFSATE	Borden
CH-124	Sea King	34	406	Shearwater
			423	Shearwater
			443	Esquimault (based at Victoria Int'l.)
CC-130E/H	Hercules	32	413	Greenwood
			429	Trenton
			436	Trenton
			435	Edmonton
CT-133	Silver Star	63	VU-32	Shearwater
			Base Flight	Bagotville
			414	North Bay
			AETE	Cold Lake
			Base Flight	Cold Lake
			VU-33	Comox
CT-134	Musketeer	19	various (ground trainers, static display)	
CT-134A	Musketeer	20	3 CFFTS	Portage la Prairie

Type	Name	Quantity	Squadrons	Base(s)
CH-135	Twin Huey	44	403	Gagetown
			430	Val Cartier
			450	Ottawa
			SERT	Ottawa
			427	Petawawa
			408	Edmonton
			AETE	Cold Lake
CH-136	Kiowa	66	403	Gagetown
			430	Val Cartier
			401	St. Hubert
			438	St. Hubert
			427	Petawawa
			400	Toronto
			411	Toronto
			408	Edmonton
			AETE	Cold Lake
			444	Lahr
CC-137	707	5	437	Trenton
CC-138	Twin Otter	7	418	Edmonton
			440	Edmonton
			440 (Det)	Yellowknife
			4 RSU	Edmonton
CH-139	Jet Ranger	14	3 CFFTS	Portage la Prairie
CP-140	Aurora	18	404	Greenwood
			405	Greenwood
			415	Greenwood
			MP & EU	Greenwood
			407	Comox
CP-140A	Arcturus*	3		Greenwood
CC-142	Dash 8	2	402	Winnipeg
CT-142	Dash 8	4	402	Winnipeg
			CFS	Winnipeg
CH-143	BK-117	1	AETE	Cold Lake
CC-144/	Challenger	15	412	Ottawa
CE-144/			AETE	Cold Lake
CP-144			414 (Det)	Shearwater
			414	North Bay
ET-133	Silver Star	9	414	North Bay
CT-145	King Air 200	2	CFS	Winnipeg
CF-188	Hornet	130	425	Bagotville
			433	Bagotville
			410	Cold Lake
			416	Cold Lake
			441	Cold Lake
			441 (Det)	Comox
			421	Baden-Soellingen
			439	Baden-Soellingen
			AETE	Cold Lake

Types deleted from flying operations 1988–91: CC-117/CE-117 Falcon (7), CP-121 Tracker (18), CC-129 Dakota (9), CH-147 Chinook (7)

*Planned delivery in late 1991 and early 1992.

AIRCOM AIRCRAFT BY SQUADRON/UNIT, September 1991

Squadron/Unit	Aircraft Flown	Squadron/Unit	Aircraft Flown
400	Kiowa	430	Kiowa, Twin Huey
401	Kiowa	431	Tutor
402	Dash 8	433	Hornet
403	Kiowa, Twin Huey	435	Hercules
404	Aurora	436	Hercules
405	Aurora	437	Boeing 707
406	Sea King	438	Kiowa
407	Aurora	439	Hornet
408	Kiowa, Twin Huey	440	Twin Otter
410	Hornet	441	Hornet
411	Kiowa	442	Buffalo, Labrador
412	Challenger, Cosmopolitan	443	Sea King
413	Hercules, Labrador	444	Kiowa
414	Challenger, T-33	2 CFFTS	Tutor
415	Aurora	3 CFFTS	Jet Ranger, Musketeer
416	Hornet	4 RSU	Twin Otter
418	Twin Otter	103 RU	Labrador
419	CF-5	AETE	CF-5, CF-18, T-33, Tutor, Challenger, Kiowa, Twin Huey, BK-117
421	Hornet		
423	Sea King	CFS	Dash 8, Jet Ranger, Musketeer, Tutor
424	Buffalo, Labrador	FIS	Jet Ranger, Musketeer, Tutor
425	Hornet	MP & EU	Aurora
426	various transports for aircrew instruction	VU-32	T-33
427	Kiowa, Twin Huey	VU-33	T-33
429	Hercules		

Announced changes in February 1991: 409 Squadron to stand down June 1991, 414 Squadron to split (half going to Comox as 414, half to Shearwater as 434). For detailed tail number lists and further appendix information, see *Canada's Air Force Today* (1987) and *CAFT - 1991 Update*, from CANAV Books.

GLOSSARY

AAM – air-to-air missile
ABDR – aircraft battle damage repair
AC – aircraft commander
AETE – Aerospace Engineering and Test Establishment
AFB – air force base
AI – airborne interception
AIRCOM – Air Command
AMC – Air Materiel Command
AMDU – Aerospace Maintenance and Development Unit
AMU – Air Movements Unit
ANG – Air National Guard
AR – aerial refuelling, Arctic reconnaissance, Air Reserve
ASW – anti-submarine warfare
ATC – Air Transport Command
ATG – Air Transport Group
ATU – Air Transport Unit
BAMEO – Base Aircraft Maintenance and Engineering Officer
"bizjet" – business jet

BGen – brigadier general
BHS – Basic Helicopter School
BOAC – British Overseas Airways Corp.
C & L – communications and liaison
CADC – Crown Assets Disposal Corp.
CAP – combat air patrol
Capt – captain
CCG – Canadian Coast Guard
CEPE – Central Experimental and Proving Establishment
CF – Canadian Forces
CFB – Canadian Forces Base
CFE – Canadian Forces Europe
CFFTS – Canadian Forces Flying Training School
CFS – Central Flying School
CFSATE – CF School of Aerospace Technology and Engineering
"chem" suit – NBCW suit
CIAS – Canadian International Air Show
"Clunk" – CF-100

CNE – Canadian National Exhibition
CO – commanding officer
Col – colonel
"comm" – communications
CP – Canadian Pacific
Cpl – corporal
Det – detachment
DFO – Department of Fisheries and Oceans
DHC – de Havilland Canada
DLIR – depot level inspection and repair
DND – Department of National Defence
dual – two seat fighter
EA – executive assistant
EW – electronic warfare
EWO – electronic warfare officer
F/L – flight lieutenant
FE – flight engineer
FG – Fighter Group
FIG – fighter interception group
FIS – Flying Instructors School
FL – flight level
FM – Fighter Meet
FO – first officer
GCI – ground controlled interception
HAS – hardened aircraft shelter
HOTEF – Helicopter Operational Test and Evaluation
    Flight
HQ – headquarters
HVAR – high velocity aircraft rocket
ICPS – Instrument Check Pilots School
IMP – International Marine Products
IPMS – International Plastic Modellers Society
KIAS – knots indicated air speed
"Lab" – Labrador
LAPES – low altitude parachute extraction system
LCol – lieutenant colonel
LGen – lieutenant general
LM – load master
"loadie" – load master
Lt – lieutenant
LWF – lightweight fighter
M – Mach
MAC – Military Airlift Command
MAD – magnetic anomaly detector
MAG – Maritime Air Group
Maj – major
MAMS – mobile air movements section

MCpl – master corporal
MEDEVAC – medical evacuation
MFO – Multinational Force and Observers
MobCom – Mobile Command
MR – maritime reconnaissance
MWO – master warrant officer
NAE – National Aeronautical Establishment
NAM – National Aviation Museum
NATO – North Atlantic Treaty Organization
NBCW – nuclear, biological and chemical warfare
NORPAT – northern patrol
NVG – night vision goggles
NWT – Northwest Territories
Ops – operations
OTU – operational training unit
panning – following a moving object with one's camera
pipeliner – a new pilot
P/O – pilot officer
Pte – private
prang – crash
QIAS – Quinte International Air Show
R-R – Rolls-Royce
RCAF – Royal Canadian Air Force
RCMP – Royal Canadian Mounted Police
RCN – Royal Canadian Navy
RWAU – Rotary Wing Aviation Unit
SAM – surface-to-air missile
SAR – search and rescue
SARTECH – search and rescue technician
SERT – special emergency response team
SF – service flight
Sgt – sergeant
SOS – struck off strength
STOL – short takeoff and landing
T-bird – Lockheed T-33
TACHEL – tactical helicopter
TALEX – tactical airlift exercise
TAM – Tactical Air Meet
TCA – Trans-Canada Air Lines
"tech" – technician
TFG – tactical fighter group
TFW – tactical fighter wing
TOS – taken on strength
u/s – unserviceable
VC – Victoria Cross
WO – warrant officer
10 TAG – 10 Tactical Air Group

LAPES action at
Mountain View,
June 8, 1991.

INDEX

A Chinook of 450 Squadron at Trenton, August 25, 1977.

1

2

3